Remodeler's Guide
¯lings

Remodeler's Guide to Suspended Ceilings

Complete instructions on selling, planning, and installing suspended ceilings

**CHICAGO
METALLIC
CORPORATION**

Library of Congress Cataloging in Publicatio

Main entry under title:

Remodeler's guide to suspended ceilings.

   Includes index.
   1. Suspended ceilings—Handbooks, manuals, etc.
2. Dwellings—Remodeling—Handbooks, manuals, etc.
I. Robert Scharff and Associates, Ltd. II. Chicago Metallic
Corporation.
TH2531.R46 1984   698   84-5008
ISBN 0-937558-04-4

10 9 8 7 6 5 4 3 2 1

Printed in the United States of America.

WI MAR '86

Dedicated to all the people who made our 90 years of service a success.

Contents

INTRODUCTION

We at Chicago Metallic Corporation are proud of the recognition and respect we hold throughout the suspended ceiling industry. Our suspended ceiling systems are examples of our basic tradition of service and quality, backed by almost a century of experience. We offer a wide selection of ceiling systems, accessories, finishes, and colors to fulfill any request, and we are constantly refining these systems and developing new ones. In addition, our systems would not have gained the popularity they have if we had not tried to follow up our products with proper installation procedures. After all, having fine products on the market is only the first step. They must also be implemented in the best manner for each situation in order to be of value to the customer.

This book is designed to help those in the installation end of the ceiling industry to best use their skills and workmanship to enhance the overall appearance and quality of the ceilings they install. We offer the contractor important information on the advantages of a suspended ceiling system as well as the necessary steps for planning, estimating, and installing a suspended ceiling. The overall purpose of this book is to combine our experience with your experience to create the best ceilings possible.

Chapter 1

WHY SUSPENDED CEILINGS?

Suspended ceilings by Chicago Metallic, one of the premier makers of roll formed suspension systems or ceiling grid, offers a most versatile and economical way to meet a great portion of remodeling and new construction finishing requirements. This book on suspended ceilings is a result of the questions and concerns many remodelers and contractors have presented to us. Chicago Metallic Corporation has designed this handbook to help both you, the contractor, and your customer get the most from suspended ceilings and our products. As the industry leader in quality and innovation, CMC needs knowledgeable contractors to provide installations and information equaling our high standards. You, as a contractor, would be wise to offer this affordable ceiling choice to your customers. Familiarize yourself with this book and discover more about how to sell to customers, better estimation techniques, the best installation procedures, and other important topics that can help increase business.

The Suspended Ceiling Advantage

As a contractor you are probably already familiar with the many advantages of suspended grid ceilings. But when confronted with a less knowledgeable client, having an organized presentation of these advantages can be an invaluable sales tool. Read the following sections carefully to clarify each point in your mind. While plaster, drywall, and other ceiling coverings are available, suspended grid ceilings are by far one of the finest overall choices in residential and commercial applications.

Plaster. Plaster work is messy and often limited by structural strength. In addition, plastering costs are high due to the need for special skilled tradesmen (Fig. 1-1) and the long periods of time required for job completion. Even after the plaster work is finished, the surface must be primed and painted.

Drywall (Plasterboard). Although the installation of a drywall ceiling is an improvement upon the application of wet plaster, it is still heavy work which requires precision to avoid poor results. Drywall ceilings must be

Fig. 1-1: *Plastering is messy and time-consuming.*

Fig. 1-2: *Drywall is heavy and requires extensive finishing.*

supported by a frame (usually wooden) which can receive nails or screws. Once hung, the plasterboard is taped, finished, primed, and painted (Fig. 1-2). Like plaster, it may split and crack with structural settling and movement.

Cemented or Stapled Tile. When installing this type of ceiling, a level, smooth attachment surface is very important because the tile takes on the configuration of the application surface (Fig. 1-3). A slow installation rate and bonding cement fumes add to an already difficult job.

Suspended Ceiling. Suspended grid and panel ceiling systems (Fig. 1-4) permit level installation without concern over the structure or type of surface covered. When discussing the suspended ceiling advantage with a customer, be sure to stress these points:

1. Growing popularity.
2. Energy savings.
3. Interior beautification.
4. Sound-deadening properties.
5. Relative inexpensiveness.

Fig. 1-3: *Cemented or stapled tile requires an extremely level surface.*

Fig. 1-4: *Suspended ceilings are easy to install and the job is completed rapidly.*

6. Installation of flush lighting and heating panels.
7. No additional finishing once installed.
8. Home/business value preservation.
9. Good product life.

Let's take a closer look at the suspended ceiling advantage.

Energy Savings. Heating and cooling costs are constantly rising. Most of your potential clients want to keep both construction and operational costs to a minimum; the suspended ceiling offers both. The moderate, one-time investment required for ceiling installation is insignificant when spread out over the lifetime of the structure. In addition, savings in heating and cooling costs will help the ceiling pay for itself.

R-value is a scale used to compare the resistance a material has to heat flow. The higher the R-value of a material, the greater the thermal resistance. Most panel manufacturers publish the R-values of their products, permitting easy comparison. Insulating requirements vary from project to project. By using different R-values for different applications, these requirements can be met. When energy savings are important, suggest a high R-value panel.

Suspended ceilings are effective insulators because their design incorporates the best insulator available, air. The plenum, or area above the level of the ceiling, provides a blanket of still air which, along with tile, reduces heating requirements. When the tile/air combination cannot meet the total insulating requirements, rock wool or fiberglass blankets can be rolled over the tiles for an additional R-value increase. Chapter 7 provides full details on insulating above the ceiling.

Acoustical Treatment. Some rooms are noisier than others. Rooms with many hard, smooth surfaces tend to bounce or reflect sound,

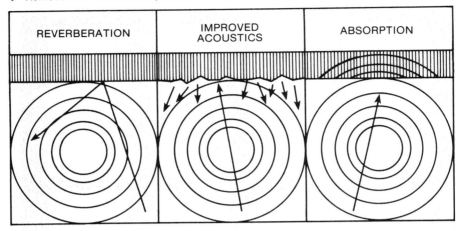

Fig. 1-5: *Acoustics can be improved through the use of suspended ceilings.*

creating an effect called reverberation (Fig. 1-5). The extreme of reverberation is what we call echo, which is undesirable in most cases. One of the most effective ways to soften sound is through suspended ceilings. Functioning as a sound sponge, acoustical tile is made to absorb sound rather than reflect it. Just as R-value varies, so does acoustical absorption. Deep-textured tile can reduce unwanted sound by up to 85% while providing a dramatic look to the room.

Many building materials possess some acoustical properties. To measure just how effective different materials are at absorbing sound, a scale called the Noise Reduction Coefficient (NRC) has been developed. The federal government has set a specification (SS-S-118A) stating that a material must possess minimum NRC of 0.40 in order to be considered acoustical. Any absorption below this level is not perceivable by the human ear. Most panel manufacturers list the NRC in their literature. Bear in mind, however, that these panels reduce reflected noise only and have no significant effect on sound transmission.

Decorative Appeal. Interior designers and architects use suspended grid ceilings because of their versatility and low maintenance. Combining grid colors and panel textures can unify a structure, yet give each area a mark of distinction. Chicago Metallic grid is available in white, black, walnut, and architectural bronze finishes. Panels, either 2′ by 4′ or 2′ by 2′, are made by several manufacturers who offer materials, textures, and colors for every need (Fig. 1-6).

The majority of panels used in residential and light commercial applications are made of either cellulose or mineral fibers. Cellulose fibers are primarily wood and/or bagasse (sugar cane fiber) that has been shredded

Fig. 1-6: *Various lay-in panel patterns.*

and formed. Mineral fibers are bonded by organic and inorganic materials and formed by felting and a heat curing process. The patterns and sound absorption properties of both types of panel are created by treating the material face in the wet stage. Color pigments, if desired, are also added at this stage. Additional pattern treatment is accomplished by mechanical means after the prepatterned product is cured.

In addition to various finishes and materials, two panel configurations, flush and reveal (or shadowline), are available (Fig. 1-7). Flush panels, as the term implies, lie even with the grid, creating a smooth ceiling. The face of the reveal edge panel hangs below the grid for a unique three-

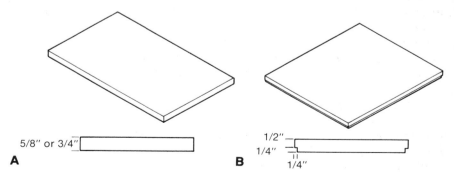

Fig. 1-7: *The two most popular panel configurations are (A) flush and (B) reveal (or shadowline).*

Fig. 1-8: *Reveal edge panels are becoming very popular in homes and commercial buildings.*

dimensional effect. A dark grid with these panels accents the dramatic visual impact. The effect enhances recreation rooms, family rooms, commercial offices, and other areas where definition of space is important (Fig. 1-8).

The wide selection of panel types and finishes permits installation in what might otherwise be a problem area. For example, certain rooms in the home (such as the kitchen, bathroom, and laundry), as well as commercial establishments (restaurants, lounges, etc.), pose a soiling problem from fumes, smoke, grease, moisture, and mildew. Acrylic-coated panels provide a cleanable surface for use in such areas. You can overcome other problem situations with the proper use of available materials.

Suspended ceilings not only look good, but also help blend accessories, such as lights, speakers, and vents, into the room. Luminous panels combined with appropriately sized fixtures can provide soft, evenly diffused light from the same plane as the ceiling. Usually constructed of non-yellowing styrene, they maintain color and brightness even when the lights are not in use. Many panel patterns are styled to match popular ceiling tile patterns.

The Chicago Metallic System Advantage

While the Chicago Metallic grid system offers clients the most for their ceiling dollar, the contractor benefits from the most important feature our system offers—installation ease. Design engineers at CMC work closely

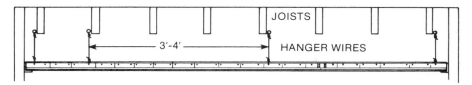

Fig. 1-9: *Hanger wire supports the system every 3' to 4'.*

with architects, interior designers, and contractors in order to determine what is needed. This responsiveness to the industry has helped us provide the finest system available.

As shown in Fig. 1-9, hanger wire every 3' to 4' supports the ceiling system. Twelve gauge wire is used in commercial installations, while lighter wire is used in residential applications. Hanger wire is secured by screw eyes in the bottom or sides of joists.

The Chicago Metallic system's grid components are strong and durable, yet light enough to permit ease of handling, field cutting, and trimming. They are electrogalvanized to resist rust and factory finished to resist chipping, scratches, and soil marks. All component finishes can be cleaned with detergent and water.

The CMC suspended ceiling system has three basic components: wall molding, main runner, and cross tee. With these components many ceiling configurations are readily available. The resulting suspended grid ceiling is a quick, no-special-tools-needed system featured in homes, business, and industry throughout the United States.

Wall Molding. The purpose of the wall molding (sometimes called wall angle) is to provide perimeter support for runners and tees. Chicago Metallic 1407 wall molding was the first on the market to provide prepunched angles for installer convenience (Fig. 1-10). Other designs require punching holes in the field or driving a nail through the component

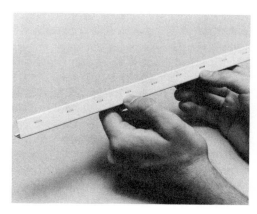

Fig. 1-10: *The Chicago Metallic 1407 wall molding was the first on the market to be prepunched for the convenience of the installer.*

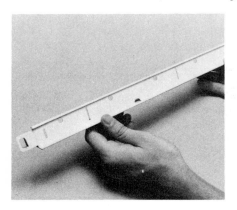

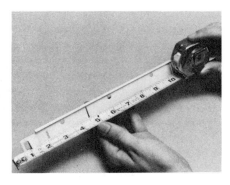

Fig. 1-12: *The 3" hanger wire hole spacing in the CMC 300 main runner design allows more direct support to keep the grid level.*

Fig. 1-11: *The Chicago Metallic 300 main runner design.*

during installation. CMC's molding is hemmed on both legs to provide rigidity and strength as well as a professionally finished look.

Main Runners. Hung by wires, these primary grid members carry most of the weight of the suspended ceiling system and interlock to provide any length. The Chicago Metallic 300 main runner design is the most advanced on the market (Fig. 1-11). Design features include:

• *Hanger holes every 3".* When component suspension holes are spread far apart (as in our competitors' products), you may have to attach hanger wires at shallow angles known as *splays.* Splaying causes a number of installation problems including lift, sag, and torqueing. Our hanger holes are placed often enough to provide direct support (Fig. 1-12), assuring a level, easy-to-install grid.

• *Cross tee slots every 6".* Slots on support components are positioned to avoid waste and increase system flexibility. Most grid sold to acoustical contractors across the United States now has this feature.

• *Easy tab splicing.* The simplicity of the CMC splicing mechanism was designed to ease main runner installation. Simply insert tabs and bend back. Unlike older click-together methods, the CMC design permits quick removal and component reuse for changes and/or replacement.

• *Either end splicing.* Chicago Metallic products have no male and female ends, making it impossible to cut off the wrong end. You can splice main runners at either end, reducing waste and time. Use trimmed ends to finish off successive main runner rows, eliminating much waste.

Cross Tees. Insert cross tees at right angles into the regularly spaced slots on the main runners. CMC cross tees (Fig. 1-13) install with a simple in-and-down motion. All tees feature hold-down tabs to secure panels once installed: another CMC pioneered design. Both 2' and 4' lengths are available. Tee location and position, as well as main runner spacing,

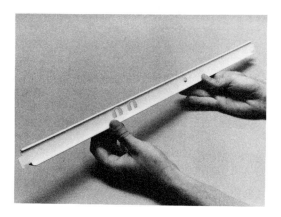

Fig. 1-13: *The Chicago Metallic cross tee design.*

allows for a wide variety of possible ceiling patterns. Chicago Metallic 300 system's cross tees are not right- or left-handed; this allows cross tee engagement on either side of the slot.

Fire Rated Ceilings

Some suspended ceiling jobs may specify that they must be fire rated. Two aspects of suspended ceilings are usually of interest to local fire prevention and building code officials: *flame spread* and *hourly rating.*

Flame spread is how fast a fire will spread over a material once the fire has touched it. To classify various fire rated materials, a numerical index has been established from the results of the American Society for Testing and Materials (ASTM) E-84 Tunnel Test. Under controlled laboratory conditions, testers measure the spread of flame across the face of a ceiling material, permitting comparison of products under identical test conditions. This test may not represent a material's performance in an actual fire. Building codes use these numbers to classify materials as follows:

Table 1-1 Flame Spread Classification

Classification	Code Designation
0-25	Class A, Class I, or Class 25
26-75	Class B, Class II, or Class 75
76-200	Class C, Class III, or Class 200
201-500	Class D, Class IV, or Class 500

Most fire rated ceiling panels fall into the Class I, or noncombustible, category. The architect or code may specify, or your customer may request, Class I materials; therefore, the material you install must have an

```
┌─────────────────────────────────────────────┐
│           ⅝" MINERAL FIBER                   │
│       ACOUSTICAL (All Sizes)                 │
│       Underwriters Laboratories Inc.®        │
│                Classified                    │
│             Acoustical Material              │
│         Surface Burning Characteristics      │
│                 Type V & D  Type IV & VI B   │
│   Flame Spread        10-15        25        │
│   Fuel Contributed    10-25        15        │
│   Smoke Developed     0-10          0        │
└─────────────────────────────────────────────┘
```

Fig. 1-14: Sample UL flame spread label.

Underwriters' Laboratories (UL) label on its packaging certifying that it is in this flame spread category (Fig. 1-14). Remember that flame spread applies to the ceiling panels only and not to the metal grid components.

The second fire code requirement, which does relate to ceiling grid, is the *hourly rating* or *time design* of the ceiling. It is usually found only in commercial construction.

The numerical time design ratings are obtained from the results of the (ASTM) E-119 Furnace Test. Under controlled laboratory conditions, testers measure the ability of a ceiling assembly to prevent the spread of fire and hot gases to the level above (floor/ceiling) or outside (roof/ceiling) and to provide protection for the structural elements to prevent early collapse. The ratings may not predict the assembly's performance in an actual fire.

Usually, time design ratings are noted as one-hour or two-hour ceiling assemblies. These terms mean that the ceiling components have been tested by Underwriters' Laboratories and hold up in fire conditions for one or two hours or longer. However, a suspended ceiling alone will *not* provide the desired protection; the composition of the structure above the suspended ceiling is even more important. To fulfill time rating requirements, consider *both* the ceiling and overhead structure.

The grid bearing fire ratings, which always carry the UL label, are not necessarily of greater strength than a standard product. Fire rated grid, however, is designed with *expansion relief sections* to prevent distortion or bending of the steel when the grid expands under fire conditions. Distortion causes ceiling panels to fall from the grid, creating openings for the fire to reach the structure above the ceiling. The purpose of a fire rated ceiling is to contain the fire and prevent or delay its reaching the overhead structure.

To contain a fire, you must use specially tested grid, such as the Chicago Metallic Fire Front system, which boasts over 63 UL tests to its credit. You must also use special fire-resistant ceiling panels which show special UL labels on their packaging. Manufacturers often give fire rated panels special brand names to highlight this feature. For ceiling panels that weigh less than 1 pound per square foot, UL codes require the installation of hold-down clips to achieve a fire rated ceiling.

Ceiling Accessories

The two most popular suspended ceiling accessories are lighting and heating units. Both are readily available in configurations suitable for in-grid use.

Lighting Units. Lighting in the ceiling can be important. You can lay pre-wired light fixture panels (Fig. 1-15) directly into grid openings of 2' by 2' and 2' by 4'. Both fluorescent and incandescent types are available.

Fluorescent Lights. Depending upon operating temperature, fluorescent lighting is usually well suited to suspended ceiling installations. You will find a wide variety of bulb and lens combinations available in the grid sizes mentioned previously. You can hang fixtures to project below the plane of the ceiling or to lie flush with the acoustical tile. Whatever the final choice, well-placed lighting can dramatically improve both room usefulness and customer satisfaction.

Incandescent Lights. Unlike fluorescent fixtures, incandescent lights are too hot for use with plastic inlay panels. Heat and weight associated with these fixtures demand their use with mineral board ceiling panels. Chicago Metallic currently manufactures an incandescent high-hat type fixture (Fig. 1-16) known as the Astralite™. This configuration comes

Fig. 1-15: *Pre-wired lighting units can be laid directly into the grid.*

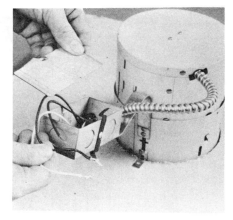

Fig. 1-16: *Chicago Metallic's Astralite™ fixture.*

already inserted in a 2′ by 2′ metal-faced panel that drops into the pre-hung grid. You can choose from white and several decorator colors. All Astralite™ fixtures are pre-wired, ready for direct attachment to house wiring.

You can find more information on the installation of lighting fixtures in Chapter 7.

Heating Units. You can use pre-wired radiant ceiling heat panels (Fig. 1-17) with either a wall switch or a thermostat. Fitting into a standard 2′ by 4′ suspended ceiling grid, the completely enclosed element provides clean, draft-free heat in hard-to-heat locations (such as doorways or seating areas next to picture windows) without ductwork or bulky radia-tors. The most modern type of construction is used. Chapter 7 gives complete installation details of a typical heating unit.

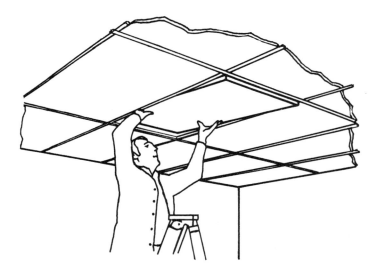

Fig. 1-17: *Pre-wired radiant heat panels install as simply as tile.*

Chapter 2

PLANNING THE JOB

Good planning is critical to the successful completion of every suspended ceiling installation since it reduces unforeseen problems that increase labor and material costs. Prior to beginning any job, take a thorough set of room measurements and draw up a detailed plan of the proposed ceiling. Have your customer select the ceiling pattern and tile desired, and calculate cost and time estimates from this information.

CHOOSING THE CEILING LAYOUT

Point out to the customer just how important their role in planning the ceiling is. As mentioned, customers have the final say in choosing the ceiling panel pattern and layout, but they can often profit from your professional advice. For example, the customer may not know that placing rectangular panels perpendicular to the length of the room can make narrow rooms appear wider, so be prepared to give advice of this nature. Careful attention to detail like this will make the work flow smoother and progress faster, ensuring you and your customer satisfaction.

The most common ceiling layout utilizes 2' by 4' panels installed perpendicular to the main runners (Fig. 2-1A). To reverse the pattern, install the panels parallel to the main runners as shown in Fig. 2-1B. To change the texture of the ceiling, you can alternate the panels to create the arrangement shown in Fig. 2-1C. Running the 2' by 4' panels in a half-

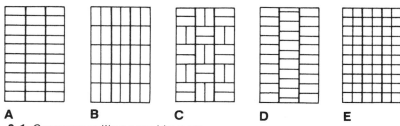

A **B** **C** **D** **E**

Fig. 2-1: Common ceiling panel layouts.

offset pattern creates the ashlar pattern in Fig. 2-1D. To achieve the 2′ by 2′ block arrangement in Fig. 2-1E, insert 2′ cross tees between the 4′ main runners.

When helping your customer select a panel pattern and texture, try to simulate occupancy lighting. If possible, avoid critical lighting, strong sidelighting that skims across the ceiling at a very slight angle, exaggerating even slight imperfections (Fig. 2-2). Where sidelighting could be a problem or where a precise installation may be difficult, employ a rough or deeply-fissured pattern rather than a smooth one. Draperies and/or blinds also help to diffuse lighting and minimize shadows.

Fig. 2-2: Strong sidelighting will exaggerate imperfections.

MEASURING THE AREA

In order to make a scale drawing, you will need the dimensions of the room or area. Take all measurements at the height of the new ceiling to avoid possible room irregularities at other levels.

Determining Ceiling Height

Ceiling height depends upon a number of variables. For example, the height of the existing ceiling and whether it is open joisted or previously finished will affect the amount of drop that can be utilized. In addition, existing lighting fixtures, ductwork, and other obstacles also affect the placement of the new installation.

In order to allow enough space necessary for insertion of the ceiling panels, maintain a minimum clearance of 3″ between the top of the main runners and the bottom of the exposed joists or obstructions such as those listed in the previous paragraph (Fig. 2-3).

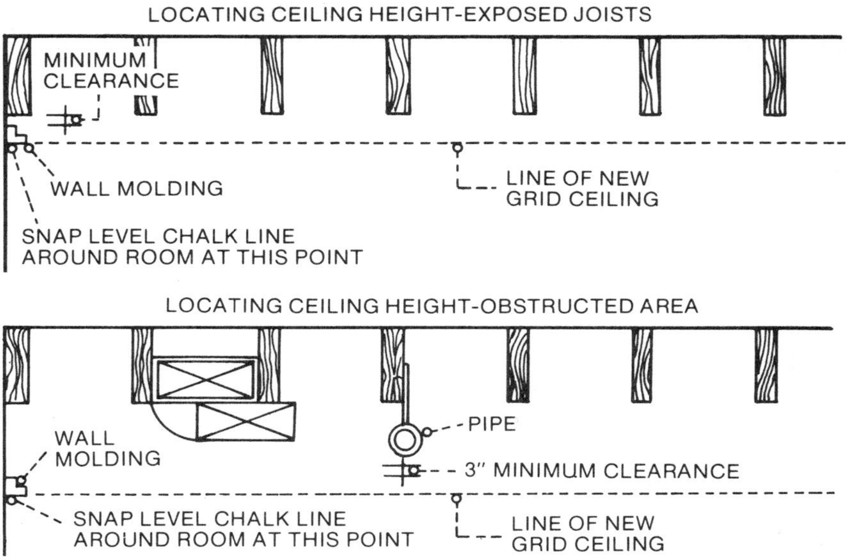

LOCATING CEILING HEIGHT-EXPOSED JOISTS

MINIMUM
CLEARANCE

WALL MOLDING

LINE OF NEW
GRID CEILING

SNAP LEVEL CHALK LINE
AROUND ROOM AT THIS POINT

LOCATING CEILING HEIGHT-OBSTRUCTED AREA

WALL
MOLDING

PIPE

3" MINIMUM CLEARANCE

SNAP LEVEL CHALK LINE
AROUND ROOM AT THIS POINT

LINE OF NEW
GRID CEILING

Fig. 2-3: *Proper clearance is important for easy installation of the ceiling panels.*

When determining lighting placement within the grid arrangement, follow the manufacturer's precautions and installation instructions to the letter. Regardless of the type of fixtures used, all electrical work (running wires or conduit, installing junction boxes, placing fixtures, etc.) should be completed prior to beginning ceiling tile installation.

Any special installation requirements must be known prior to determining ceiling height. For example, different accessories dictate certain minimum clearance considerations: storage compartments, at least 9", and blanket insulation, 6".

Determining Joist Direction

The main runners for the Chicago Metallic suspended ceiling systems are usually hung from ceiling joists. Since main runners are designed to run perpendicular to ceiling joists, you must determine the direction in which the joists run. This task is simple in rooms where the ceiling joists are exposed. However, if the joists are covered with plaster or drywall, determining their location and running direction may be a more difficult task.

You can usually locate a joist by lightly tapping the ceiling with a hammer and noting the hollow and solid sounds. A hollow sound means there is no joist; a solid sound indicates the presence of a joist. To be certain, drill several small holes side by side in the ceiling until you bore into the joist. A magnetic stud finder can also locate joists.

Ceiling joists are usually placed 16" or 24" apart on centers (O.C.); therefore, once you accurately locate one, you can find the others by measuring. Also keep in mind that joists usually run parallel to a room's shorter walls.

MAKING THE SCALE DRAWING

After determining a ceiling pattern and layout, a scale drawing must be prepared. A set of blueprints are neither practical nor needed for every installation, yet some plan is required for estimating and clarifying any field questions. The layout sketch must clearly indicate room outline, ceiling pattern layout, and location and direction of joists. Indicate every irregularity and obstruction exactly to scale: alcoves, bays, columns, stairways, beams, lighting units, speakers, grilles, vents, and so on. Also note the location of doors and windows.

Graph paper is essential when preparing a scaled layout. Each square represents 1' or 2', depending upon room size (Fig. 2-4).

First, draw the outline of the room; include every irregularity and obstruction. Next, in heavy lines or colored pencil, draw the main runners at right angles to the joists on 4' centers. Draw the first runner on the room centerline when possible; when it is not possible, draw it 1' to 2' from the

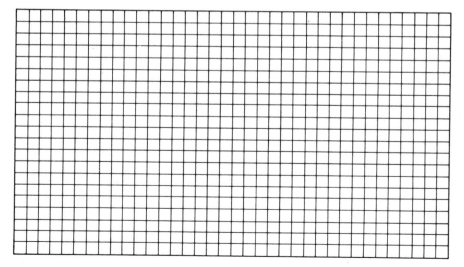

Fig. 2-4: *Using graph paper will allow you to more easily make a scale drawing.*

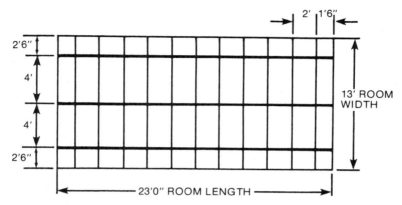

Fig. 2-5: *Laying out a suspended ceiling plan.*

centerline. This yields the widest possible border tile width. The rule of thumb for border tile width is to always make the border more than half the tile width. For example, although a room 13' wide could be handled by using three 4' wide tiles and a 6" border on each side, consider the alternate treatment using the rule of thumb (Fig. 2-5): two 4' panels with 2-1/2' borders. Figure 2-6 shows that reversing the standard installation pattern can give width to a narrow room.

Next, add cross tees at right angles to the main runners. When working with 2' by 4' panels, space the 2' cross tees on 2' centers perpendicular to and between the 4' cross tees. If a 2' by 2' panel is chosen, the main runner spacing and cross tee placement are on 2' centers. Cross tee intervals follow the same border width rule as main runners. Try to use the centerline of the room as a starting point whenever possible. Sometimes, however, it is impossible to follow the rule for border width if a specific lighting fixture or other design consideration makes a small border unavoidable.

Determining Border Tile Width

While most suspended ceiling areas are rectangular in shape, sometimes you will encounter rooms of odd proportions (Fig. 2-7). In these cases, plan around the intersecting centerlines in order to achieve a ceiling that is balanced over the largest, most visible portion of the ceiling.

Reflected ceiling plans may indicate centerline and specify width of border units. These guidelines should always be followed when provided. Often, however, establishment of centerlines and planning the ceiling layout for even border tiles may be left up to the acoustical ceiling installer. In such instances border tile width should be the same on facing

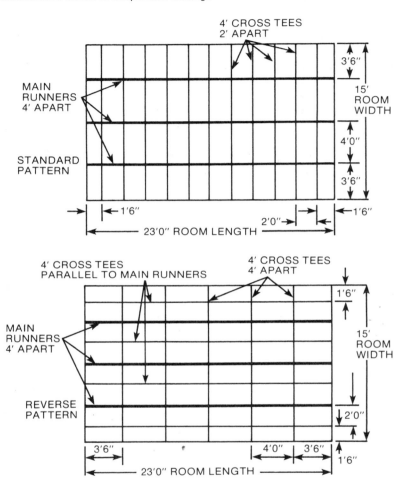

Fig. 2-6: *Standard and reverse pattern layouts.*

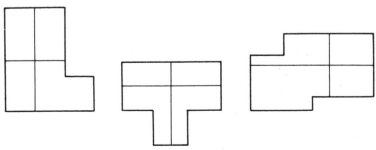

Fig. 2-7: *Typical irregular rooms.*

walls, with the tiles not less than one-half the size of a full tile. Border tile width may be determined by the following method.

Since the dimensions of the room are known, the calculation of the border tile width is easily made from these figures. The first step is to divide the room dimension exactly in half. The result is then divided by the tile dimension parallel to the room wall. If the remainder is less than half a tile width, one-half the tile dimension is added to this number. The result of this addition is the border width.

For example, a grid ceiling is to be installed in a room measuring 56'6" by 36'6", using 2' by 2' ceiling tiles. What should the width of the border tiles running parallel to the long wall be? The correct answer is found in the following manner:

$$\text{room dimension} \div 2 = \text{centerline}$$
$$56'6'' \div 2 = 28'3''$$
$$\text{centerline} \div \text{tile dimension} = \text{tiles}$$
$$28'3'' \div 2 = 14 \text{ tiles placed every } 2' + 3'' \text{ remainder}$$

The tile width is 2'. Since 3" is less than half this measurement, one-half the tile width must be added.

$$\text{\# of inches (if less than 1/2 tile)} + 1/2 \text{ tile width} = \text{border width}$$
$$3'' + 12'' = 15''$$

This particular installation will use 27 full tiles with 15" borders against each long wall (Fig. 2-8). To find the border width for the other walls,

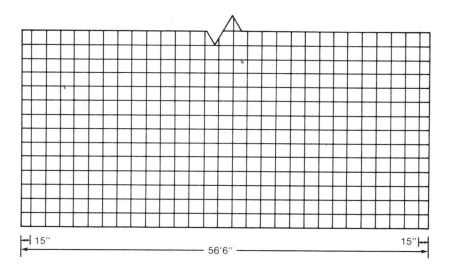

| 15" | 56'6" | 15" |

Fig. 2-8: *Properly adjusted border tiles.*

simply repeat this procedure using the other dimension as a base figure. *Note:* When the border width is adjusted, make sure to subtract one tile from the number of whole tiles to compensate for border distribution.

If recessed, built-in lighting is to be installed, decide where these luminous panels will be located and clearly identify them on the drawing. Fluorescent fixtures give more than three times the light of comparable incandescent fixtures. However, there are many instances where incandescent light fixtures are desirable. Any lighting panels and any ceiling heating panels desired must be called for on the ceiling plan. In other words, everything that is necessary to complete the ceiling installation must be included on your scaled drawing.

Using Reflected Ceiling Plans and Shop Drawings

On some installation jobs, especially when blueprints are provided, a reflected ceiling plan may be used to show construction detail. Such drawings are done to scale and show, in an artistic manner, what the finished project will look like.

These plans differ slightly from scale drawings. Reflected ceiling plans are professionally prepared and view the installation from the floor upward. Scale drawings, while accurate, are rough overhead views concerned with locating support mechanics. Shop drawings, yet another type, show specific details of installation techniques or unique architectural designs requiring special attention. Both reflected ceiling plans and shop drawings are provided to make the job proceed smoothly. Proper knowledge and utilization of blueprints and the related drawings will enable you to perform the finest possible installation and avoid problems.

Checking Blueprints

Before starting work on a job site, check the construction documents against the physical structure. The following points should be considered.

1. *Look at the room schedule.* If no one is available to instruct you in a section of a new building, check the room schedule for the type of ceiling to be installed and the panels required.

2. *Locate the room on the floor plan.* If a discrepancy exists as to dimensions, check the scale.

3. *Verify the scale.* Be sure to use the correct scale and double-check the room dimensions.

4. *Check for a ceiling plan.* If no ceiling plan exists, try to locate the working drawing to aid in the specifics of installation.

5. *Make sure the blueprint you are checking is up to date.* Often blueprints are revised before the ceiling is ready for installation. Make sure the blueprint date matches the one on the worksheet. If work already done does not conform with specifications on the blueprint, check for the final revision blueprint.

6. *Be sure the ceiling to be installed conforms with the specifications.* If the ceiling seems to be in conflict with the specifications, double-check with the supervisor.

7. *Refer to mechanical and electrical drawings before laying out the ceiling.* The location of other fixtures will affect ceiling installation. Be familiar with the other phases of construction.

8. *Make your ceiling plan.* If a separate ceiling plan is not available, it is a good idea to make one. Instead of taking the measurements yourself, use the dimensions given on the blueprint to make your scaled drawing of the grid system and panel layout.

Chapter 3

ESTIMATING THE JOB

For the contractor, one of the most important phases of any suspended ceiling job is estimating. Your two basic goals on every project are professionally completed work and a realized profit. Estimating is often the difference between financial success and failure. Experience is the key to estimating success, but neither this book nor any other can give you experience, only advice. The best instruction for estimating is *consistency in method and record*. Prepare each estimate the same way and keep every job on file. The guidelines below cover the basic considerations for estimating a suspended grid installation.

ESTIMATING MATERIAL

After drawing the suspended ceiling plan, you can easily figure out the components and materials necessary to complete the job.

Wall Molding

To find the amount of wall molding needed, first determine the perimeter of the room by adding the length of each wall section together. Then divide the room perimeter by the molding section length. Add one section for any fractions obtained.

Example: The number of 10' wall molding sections required for an installation measuring 23' by 25' would be as follows:

$$\text{(wall width + wall length)} \times 2 = \text{linear feet}$$
$$(23' + 25') \times 2 = 96'$$
$$\text{linear feet} \div \text{section length} = \text{number of sections}$$
$$96' \div 10' = 9.6 \approx 10$$

Ten sections of 10' wall molding are needed to complete this ceiling project.

Main Runners

Use the area of a given location to determine the number of main runners required for a job. Because 250 linear feet of main runner are necessary for every 1,000 square feet of area on 4' centers, you can determine main runner requirements using the following formula:

square footage of area ÷ on center (O.C.) spacing of main runner = linear footage of main runner

Example: If the square footage of a sample room is 575 square feet (23' by 25'), the number of main runners on 4' centers would be:

575 ÷ 4 = 143.75 linear feet

Divide this number by the length of the sections to be used.

143.75 ÷ 12 = 11.98 or 12, 12' main runners

A total of 12, 12' main runners are needed to cover this ceiling.

Cross Tees

Like main runners, cross tee requirements may be calculated on the basis of area. When 4' cross tees are used to create a 2' by 4' grid, 500 linear feet of tees are required for every 1,000 square feet of area. When 2' cross tees are used in conjunction with 4' cross tees to form 2' square grid openings, an additional 250 linear feet of 2' cross tees are needed for every 1,000 square feet of area. The following calculations are based on the sample room of 575 square feet.

4' Grid (4' cross tees):

square footage of area ÷ O.C. spacing of 4' cross tees = linear feet of 4' cross tees

575 ÷ 2 = 287.5 linear feet

linear feet ÷ cross tee length = number of cross tees

287.5 ÷ 4 = 71.875 or 72, 4' cross tees

2' Grid (4' cross tees and 2' cross tees):

From the calculations above, you can see that 72, 4' cross tees are needed for this 575 square foot room. To calculate the number of 2' cross tees required to form 2' square grids, proceed as follows:

square footage of area ÷ O.C. spacing of 2' cross tees = linear feet of 2' cross tees

575 ÷ 2 = 287.5 linear feet

linear feet ÷ cross tee length = number of cross tees

287.5 ÷ 2 = 143.75 or 144, 2' cross tees

Therefore, you need 72, 4' cross tees and 144, 2' cross tees to construct a 2' square grid panel configuration in a ceiling area of 575 square feet.

Note: When using area formulas such as these for determining material requirements, bear in mind that these estimates are not exact. They are educated guesses or rules of thumb, and if carefully followed, enough materials will be on hand to finish the job.

Ceiling Panels

Depending upon the installation size, one of two calculations is commonly used. For larger jobs, determine the area of the ceiling; then deduct the square footage occupied by whole panel accessories (lights, heating panels, vents, etc.) from this figure. Divide the net whole panel area by the area of one ceiling panel.

Example: The sample installation is 29' by 36'. The whole panel area is 24' by 36' (Fig. 3-1). Two-foot by 4' panels are to be used with one dozen 2' by 4' lighting fixtures. There is a row of border tiles measuring 2' by 30" running along the 36' walls.

short wall whole panel width ×
long wall whole panel length = sq ft whole panel area
24 × 36 = 864 sq ft of whole panel area
number of light fixtures × area of fixture = total accessory square footage
12 × (2 × 4) = 96
whole panel area − accessory area = net area
864 − 96 = 768
net area ÷ area of panel = number of whole panels
768 ÷ 8 = 96

The number of border panels required is determined using the border panel size and number. Count the border panels along one wall. If the dimension of the border panel is a half panel or less, order this number plus 10 tiles. If the dimension is more than a half panel width, multiply the border count by 2 and add to the total.

Example: 18 border panels measuring 2-1/2' by 2' run parallel to the 36' room wall,

number of border panels × 2 = total panels for border
18 × 2 = 36

For the sample installation, the total panel count would be:

Whole tiles 96
Border tiles 36
Total 132, 2' by 4' tiles

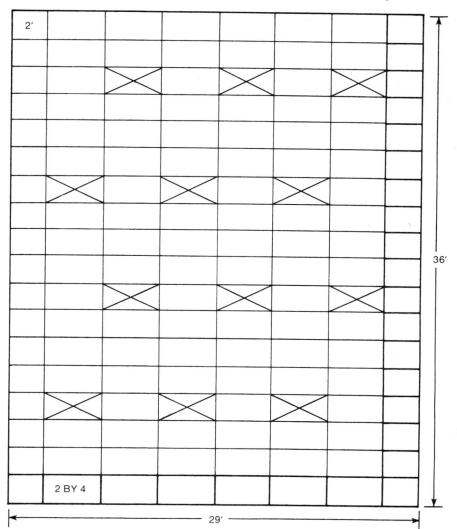

2'

2 BY 4

36'

29'

Fig. 3-1: *Note the whole panel area in this sample illustration.*

When working with smaller rooms, the method just described is not necessary. Simply count the number of full panels along a short and a long wall. If the border panel width is one-half or more, count it as a whole panel; if not, figure two borders per panel. Multiply these numbers to yield the total number of panels required. For every panel sized accessory, subtract one from the number. Remember, you are working with the number of panels, not their area.

Suspension Materials

In addition to actual grid hardware, you must order installation supplies such as hanger wire and fasteners. Either a screw eye or 10-penny nail is required to attach each hanger wire to the ceiling. You also need wall molding fasteners, which are usually nails but vary with construction materials and joist types.

Hanger Wire. Hanger wires are attached to main runners at 4' intervals. In commercial installations, use at least 12 gage hanger wire. Local building codes will usually specify gage requirements according to seismic or regional conditions. Determine the number of hanger wires in the following manner:

Example: In the sample room with an area of 575 square feet, 12 sections of 12' main runner are required. The number of hanger wires is found as follows:

$$\text{number of main runners} \times$$
$$\text{number of wires per runner (1 every 3')} = \text{number of required hanger wires}$$
$$12 \times 3 = 36 \text{ hanger wires}$$

Cut these wires 1' longer than the difference between the old and new ceiling height in order to allow 6" for a top wrap and 6" for a bottom wrap. To determine the appropriate length of hanger wire needed for a given area, multiply the correct length by the number of wires determined above plus the number of wires required to support accessories.

Example: The total amount of hanger wire needed for a room using 36 hanger wires to suspend a ceiling 2' below the existing ceiling is:

$$\text{ceiling drop} + 1' = \text{single wire length}$$
$$2' + 1' = 3' \text{ hanger wire}$$
$$\text{single wire length} \times \text{number of wires} = \text{total hanger wire}$$
$$3' \times 36 = 108 \text{ linear feet}$$

Add 10% to accommodate for cutting and mistakes.

Hanger Wire Insert. You will need one attachment point (hanger wire insert) for each wire. Use the same number as determined for required hanger wires.

Wall Molding Fasteners. To determine the proper amount of fasteners needed to attach the wall molding to the wall, simply divide the linear feet of molding by 1.33 and add 10%.

$$\text{linear feet of wall molding} \div 1.33 = \text{number of fasteners}$$
$$96 \div 1.33 = 72.1 \text{ or } 72 \text{ fasteners}$$
$$72 + 7 = 79 \text{ fasteners}$$

Light Fixtures

Count the quantity of light fixtures and types in the scale drawing. Be sure to consider special conditions required to meet fire codes. Purchase the lights when the ceiling material is bought to permit uninterrupted installation. Full details on the installation of light fixtures are given in Chapter 7.

Luminous Panels. Each fluorescent light fixture requires a luminous panel. Incandescent lighting is not recommended with such panels because of higher operating temperatures.

Estimation Form

Keep the total materials take-off for every job on a standardized form. Make any notes on estimating problems and use these sheets for future reference. Following a procedure of record keeping will result in more consistent estimates with time. A typical estimating form that can be used is shown in Fig. 3-2.

ESTIMATE SUMMARY								
PROJECT	Don Mell Assocs.		TOTAL AREA	XXX sq. ft.		SHEET NO.	I	
LOCATION	2820 Byard Blvd.		COST PER S.F.	$xx		ESTIMATE NO.	443	
CLIENT	B. Smith		COST PER L.F.	$xx		DATE	2/28/84	
ESTIMATED BY	J. Flugle		CHECKED BY	Dave Drewster				

SITE WORK

NO.	DESCRIPTION	MATERIAL	LABOR	SUBCONTR.	TOTAL	ADJUSTMENT
XXX	hanger wire inserts	X OO	XX OO		XX OO	XX OO
XXX	molding fasteners	X OO	XXX OO		XX OO	XX OO
XXX	12' wall molding	XX OO	XXX OO		XXX OO	XX OO
XXX	12 gage hanger wire	XX OO	XXX OO		XXX OO	XXX OO
XXX	12' main runners	XXX OO	XXX OO		XXX OO	XXX OO
XXX	4' cross tees	XX OO	XX OO		XX OO	XXX OO
XXX	2' x 4' ceiling panels	XXX OO	XX OO		XX OO	XX OO
	PAGE TOTAL					$ XXXXX OO

Fig. 3-2: *A typical estimating form.*

LABOR COSTS

While it is possible to give an accurate estimate on materials used for a suspended ceiling job, it is much more difficult to figure labor costs. It is almost impossible to measure the average productivity of an individual. Once you know how well you and your crew work together, you can estimate how long it will take you to finish a job.

The installation of a suspended ceiling is a fairly easy procedure, especially when following the details given in the upcoming chapters. As you and your personnel become familiar with the steps of installation, the task of putting up a suspended ceiling will be easier, installation time will be greatly decreased, and labor costs reduced.

Sources in the acoustical industry have provided Chicago Metallic with a fairly accurate, approximate percentage of work time for each of the major steps involved in suspended ceiling installation. During the installation of a suspended ceiling, the largest amount of time, between 45% and 50%, is spent on room layout, aligning the wall molding and installing hanger wires. Between 30% and 35% of the installation time is spent cutting and installing main runners and cross tees. The remaining work time is devoted to installing ceiling panels. These figures indicate that the majority of time is spent aligning and installing main runners and cross tees. The Chicago Metallic system's design makes this task easy, and it is still durable enough to match the most exacting industry standards.

When estimating labor costs, be on the lookout for construction problems. Chapter 6 gives details on some of the hidden problems you may face in making a suspended ceiling installation. For instance, duct vents may be needed if the level of the new ceiling is below existing vents. All ductwork must be done in accordance with appropriate local building code guidelines, and you must figure any special labor costs in your estimate. In any event, air ducts and vents must not rest any weight on the ceiling grid; they should be supported by their own independent suspension. Be sure to estimate both material and labor for such special installation tasks.

Chapter 4

BEFORE STARTING A JOB

Before beginning any extensive planning or actual physical work, check the installation site for proper working conditions. Since it may require hours or even days to alleviate some types of improper conditions, have the work site checked well in advance.

WORKING CONDITIONS

Before you install a suspended ceiling in either a residential or light commercial structure, make certain the following working conditions exist in order to ensure a satisfactory installation.

Preparation

Prior to installation, make sure that all wet-installed material (plaster, ceramic tile, concrete, etc.) is in place and thoroughly dried; windows are installed and glazed; all exterior doors are hung; and the roof is weathertight.

Have electrical and mechanical trades complete all their work above the ceiling line before you and your crew start work. Where ductwork is so extensive that wire hanger installation is impossible, provide for proper framing of adequate strength to support the grid. If other trades must complete any work after the ceiling is in place (for example, installing recessed, surface, or suspended fixtures), it is their responsibility to do so without damaging the acoustical installation or distorting its level.

Humidity and Temperature

The humidity and temperature before and during ceiling installation should be as close as possible to the humidity and temperature anticipated during home or building occupancy.

The ideal temperature range for ceiling installation is between 60°F and 85°F, with 45°F and 120°F being the extremes. Whenever possible, avoid temperature extremes because they affect metal component size. Seemingly small changes in component length can distort an installation, especially after climate conditions are stabilized. Grid components, in series, compound elongation or contraction problems. High humidity is also detrimental to installation. In general, do not install panels in humidity higher than 80%.

If at all possible, use the heating or cooling system (depending upon the season) to obtain proper installation conditions. If no systems are working, a temporary source of climate control is advisable. When the heating/cooling system utilizes a pressurized plenum, the ventilating system should be in operation at least 48 hours before the ceiling installation begins; this is to ensure that dust and dirt are blown out of the system. Failure to take this precaution may lead to soiling of the installed ceiling panels.

To prevent condensation and related ceiling stains, make sure the roof deck is well ventilated and properly insulated with an effective vapor barrier. Under normal occupancy humidity, you can lay insulating blankets over the grid (maximum of 0.75 pounds per square foot to prevent sag). Overlaid insulation reduces plenum access ease, but it does not eliminate the need for above-ceiling ventilation. Chapter 7 contains additional insulating information.

The acoustical contractor should not be responsible for an installation where proper humidity and temperature requirements are not maintained before, during, and after the installation.

Cleanliness of the Work Area

The installation site should be broom clean. Other trades are responsible for leaving the work site clean and free of equipment and materials that could hamper your activity. Upon completion of your work, make sure the same broom clean conditions exist.

Light and Power

Adequate lighting and electrical power supplies are mandatory for proper installation of a suspended ceiling. If natural light is insufficient, use supplementary artificial light. Lighting must be generous, and it should simulate final room lighting to check its effect on the panels.

Power outlets within 100' of the work site are essential to uninterrupted installation progress. Locate outlets when taking measurements of the installation site, noting any special needs such as extension cords, adapters, etc.

HANDLING AND STORAGE OF MATERIALS

All suspended ceiling products are fragile. Handle and stack cartons carefully (Fig. 4-1), as rough handling will cause chipping and breakage. Do not use cartons of panels as a ladder or scaffolding. Use damaged tile at locations where tile must be cut; make minor repairs with paint. Store ceiling materials in areas protected from the elements and excessive moisture. Well before beginning installation, store materials under temperature and humidity conditions identical to those on the job to avoid future problems of warpage, shrinkage, and expansion.

Fig. 4-1: Handle and stack cartons carefully.

INSTALLATION TOOLS

Most of the tools needed (Fig. 4-2) for the installation of a suspended ceiling are already in your toolbox. These include the following hand tools.
Aviation snips
Combination square
Dry lines (reference strings)
Hacksaw
Utility (tile) knife

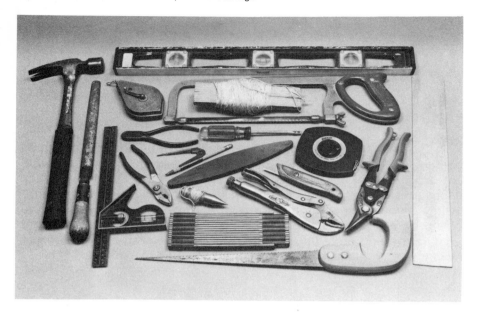

Fig. 4-2: *Important hand tools used in suspended ceiling installation.*

Screwdriver
Wire nippers
50′ (or 100′) Steel tape
6′ Carpenter's level
Plumb bob
Chalk line
Clamping pliers (vise grips)
Claw hammer
Honing stone
Straightedge
Keyhole saw
6′ Folding or push-pull rule
Wood rasp
Compass or scribe
Water level

Water Level. The water level (Fig. 4-3) is simply a long, clear tube filled with tinted water. Rubber stops or clamps permit storage and easy transportation without the need to drain and refill the level at every job. A water level is simple to construct. Obtain an appropriate length of clear 1/2″ flexible tubing (50′ or longer), and fill with water dyed by food coloring and treated with enough chlorine to retard growth of algae. Do

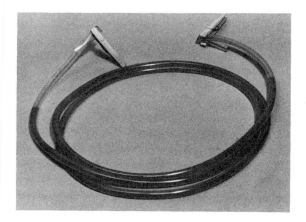

Fig. 4-3: *The water level.*

not completely fill the tube; leave 3" to 4" of open tube at each end. Make sure all air bubbles are out of the tube to ensure level accuracy. When using your water level, pinch the ends shut in order to prevent spillage during transport. For best results, use the level in the following manner:

1. Place one bench mark on the wall near the corner at eye level (approximately 5' to 6').

2. Hold the water level against the wall at this bench mark. (*Note:* At least 3" of tube should extend above the bench mark.)

3. Have your partner take the other end of the water level to the far side of the same wall and hold it at approximately the same height.

4. Now keep your eye on your bench mark while he adjusts his end of the hose by raising or lowering it.

5. When the level of water is at the same height as your bench mark, tell him to mark this point on the wall.

6. He can now move his end of the hose to another wall and proceed to set bench marks on it in a similar manner.

Aviation Snips. Use aviation snips to cut or trim steel grid components. Designed with a special cutting action, these snips require minimum effort to operate. Most feature a spring action that opens the snips after a cut has been made. Bear these points in mind when using your aviation snips:

1. Start your cuts right on your guide lines.

2. Insert the snips over the suspension member as far as possible. You control your cuts better when cutting near the throat rather than near the blade tips (Fig. 4-4).

3. Avoid tilting your snips as you cut; tilting the blades will pinch the metal and create burrs.

4. Stop each stroke a safe distance from the blade tips. Do not snap tips together; this will bend the metal.

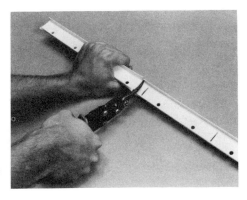

Fig. 4-4: *Proper aviation snips cutting technique.*

5. Be careful not to extend your cuts too far into the metal.

6. Always keep your snips well oiled and properly adjusted. If the blades become loose, they will not cut properly.

7. Never use snips as a hammer or screwdriver.

8. Do not attempt to cut heavy gage metals with these snips.

9. Never toss snips into your toolbox. This may damage blades.

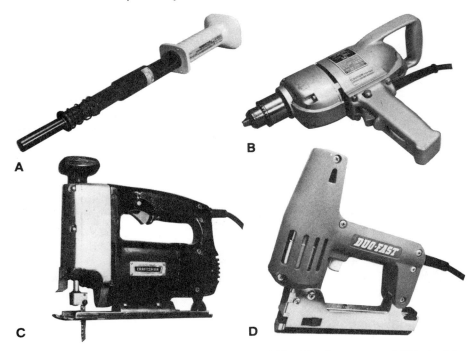

Fig. 4-5: *The (A) power fastener, (B) electric drill, (C) saber saw, and (D) electric hammer are four helpful power tools.*

Almost any technique for cutting metal will raise burrs on the trimmed ends; therefore, use a metal file to remove burrs kicked up in trimming.

Electric or Power Tools. The following electric or power tools are helpful, but not necessary, in the installation of a suspended ceiling (Fig. 4-5):

Power fastening tool (power hammer)
1/4" or 3/8" Electric drill
Saber saw
Electric hammer

In many cases, one of the first steps in the actual installation of a suspended ceiling is driving the hanger inserts into a reinforced concrete structure. If you use eye pins, you must utilize a power fastening tool (power hammer) to shoot them into the ceiling. Handle this tool (Fig. 4-6) with extreme care. Follow manufacturer's instructions to the letter in loading and firing. *Note:* A valid power hammer license is required to operate these devices in some areas. Check local building codes and city ordinances concerning their use.

In general, to load the power fastening tool:
1. Set the eye pin into the rear of the barrel.
2. Place the breech into position.
3. Insert the cartridge shell into the rear of the breech.
4. Install the trigger mechanism and lock it in place.

To fire the mechanism:
1. Butt the power fastening tool against the ceiling at the desired location for the eye pin.
2. Depress the gun by pushing against the handle. *Note:* As a safety feature, this tool will not fire unless it has been fully depressed.
3. Strike the end of the tool with a hammer. The explosion of the cartridge shell drives the eye pin securely into the ceiling.

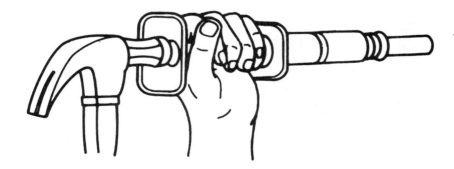

Fig. 4-6: *Proper handling of a power hammer is important.*

An electric hammer also allows you to drive various types of inserts, such as star anchors, into ceilings. With a star drill adapter, this tool can install anchor wing toggle assemblies into clay tile blocks. In those localities where power fastening tools are banned, use an electric hammer as a substitute.

Specialty Tools. One specialty tool that comes in handy is the pop-rivet gun. By pop-riveting some of the main runners to the wall molding, you can prevent a large suspended ceiling from drifting. Accepted practice is to pop-rivet every other main runner to the wall molding, but only after you have made sure that both the main runners and the cross tees have been installed perpendicularly to each other (Fig. 4-7). We at Chicago Metallic recommend that you pop-rivet main runners only to two adjacent walls. This prevents buckling of the ceiling should there be any significant rise in the temperature, causing expansion of metal parts.

To pop-rivet grid members together:

1. Punch a hole into two members at their junction.
2. Place the rivet into the mouth of the gun.
3. Insert the rivet into the hole.
4. Squeeze the handle of the pop-rivet gun.

The easiest way to punch holes in grid members is with a whitney punch (Fig. 4-8). When you have two metal members in correct alignment, ease the punch over them and squeeze on the handle to make your hole.

Ladders and scaffolding are essential to ceiling installation because they enable you to work at the proper level. Many people use two ladders and two 2″ by 6″ planks as scaffolding for small jobs, but the so-called commercial setup or patent scaffolds (Fig. 4-9) are safer and easier to use.

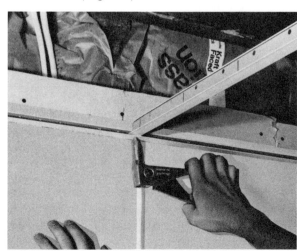

Fig. 4-7: *Pop-rivet components to wall molding.*

Fig. 4-8: *The whitney punch.*

Fig. 4-9: *Scaffolding simplifies ceiling installation.*

The scaffold unit used most frequently by residential and light commercial contractors is the 6′ by 30″ size; however, scaffolding is also available in 8′ by 30″ and 10′ by 30″ models. These units provide platforms for work done at heights from 8′ to 12′. Generally, you will need two scaffold levels for suspended ceiling work. Set the upper level at the height that will permit the installer to drive inserts into the ceiling and connect hanger wires to them. Set the lower level so that the grid and panel can be easily handled.

To erect a setup scaffold unit for large, high areas, bear the following points in mind:

1. The uprights must be plumb lined to be sure they are straight.
2. Be sure to fasten the kicker arms securely. Hammer the hooks into the framing mechanism with a few strong blows. *Note:* When ready to move an erected platform, check to see in what direction the A-frame jacks face. Be sure to move the scaffold in the same direction to reduce the chances of toppling the frame.

Have a ladder on almost every job because scaffolding, no matter how extensive, usually does not cover the entire area. Areas too small for scaffolding or areas obstructed by irregularities all require the use of ladders. Be sure to use only a heavy-duty commercial ladder (Fig. 4-10) for these purposes.

Fig. 4-10: *A heavy-duty industrial ladder provides the best combination of mobility and safety.*

Chapter 5

BASIC SUSPENDED CEILING INSTALLATIONS

The procedures for installing suspended grid ceiling in both residential and light commercial settings are quite similar. Commercial installations usually cover a larger area, so some special installation techniques may be needed. A clear understanding of blueprints and careful coordination of work performed by other trades are essential when installing commercial ceilings. Check the architect's take-off sheet for special instructions before beginning work and make certain the ceiling is installed in the proper room.

In most cases, a single worker can install an exposed grid ceiling. An assistant may be needed for larger jobs or unique situations. Chicago Metallic grid is easy to install, but to ensure trouble-free work and the finest results possible, always follow the basic installation guidelines outlined in this chapter.

Marking New Ceiling Height

Often, before actual work can begin, scaffolding must be erected to the desired work height; a ladder works well in smaller installation areas. It is then possible to mark the height of the ceiling being installed. Remember to always double-check your clearance calculations before marking any final ceiling height marks.

To find the new ceiling height, first set bench marks at the same exact height in all corners of the room. Because the floor and ceiling are not level in all parts of a given room, you should never use them as reference points from which to make bench mark measurements. Instead, establish accurate bench marks on each of the four walls by using a water level (see Chapter 4) or carpenter's level.

Utilize this same technique to establish bench marks on the remaining walls and on all protruding wall surfaces (Fig. 5-1). Use these bench marks as reference points from which to measure up to the desired ceiling height. Remember to add 3/4" to this measurement to account for wall molding width (Fig. 5-2). For example, if bench marks have been set at a

39

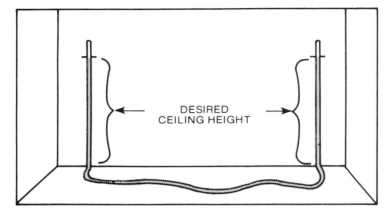

Fig. 5-1: *Establish bench marks on each wall surface.*

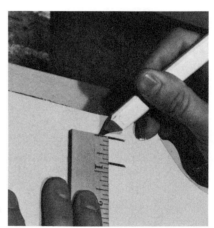

Fig. 5-2: *Add 3/4" to the ceiling height to compensate for wall molding width.*

height of 5' on all walls and a finished ceiling height of 8' is desired, measure up a distance of 3'3/4" from all bench marks and make ceiling height marks at 8'3/4" on all walls. Snap a chalk line at this height.

It is best to have an assistant help you snap the chalk line, but there is a short cut you can use when working alone. Once the ceiling height marks have been accurately established, hammer a small finishing nail into the wall at one of these ceiling height marks and tie the end of the chalk line to it. Carefully extend the line the entire length of the wall, and align it to a second ceiling height mark. You can now snap the chalk line. Be sure the line is correctly aligned with the ceiling height marks before snapping it. Never snap a chalk line that will not be covered by the completed installation.

When the ceiling molding is installed, it will cover all chalk lines and effectively lower ceiling height 3/4" to the correct 8' height. That is why it is extremely important to align the top edge of the wall molding along this chalk line. (For moldings other than CMC 1407, use the back leg dimension in place of the 3/4" used here.)

Use a carpenter's level in smaller rooms to establish bench marks. Also use a carpenter's level in place of a chalk line when drawing the final ceiling height reference line on the walls. This method is slow, partially because of many trips up and down the ladder. Striking lines using the water level and chalk line method is still preferred.

Fastening Wall Molding

Once the ceiling height line has been established, the wall molding strips can be installed. As mentioned, it is extremely important to align the top edge of the molding with the chalk line (Fig. 5-3). Nail through the prepunched molding holes into the wall studs using 6d nails. Nail both ends of the strip; check the strip for levelness and complete nailing into every stud. Chicago Metallic's wall molding has more prepunched molding holes (every 1-3/8") than any other wall molding. This eliminates the need to realign holes or custom punch holes, both time-consuming tasks.

Begin work in one corner and work around the room in an orderly manner. If wall studs cannot be located, use molly fasteners for support. Screw anchors, concrete nails, or other masonry fasteners hold in brick and other masonry walls; rawl plugs and tappets should be used in glazed tile and similar materials. Double-check the molding with a carpenter's level for best results.

Fig. 5-3: *Install the wall molding when it is aligned with the chalk line.*

Fig. 5-4: *Corner treatment.*

Handling Corners

Inside and outside corners are formed with aviation snips or a fine-toothed hacksaw. Use a standard miter box with a metal saw to miter inside and outside corners. This method produces the most professional-looking corner treatment (Fig. 5-4), although several simpler methods are often used. A 45° angle can be cut on one molding piece and the intersecting section trimmed square to the wall. Place the half miter underneath the trimmed piece to give a mitered look.

When a miter box is not available, use a combination square to mark "V" miters or 45° cuts. Only four steps are involved:

1. Measure and mark the location for the "V" cut. (Be sure to consider corner bead angles; however, these angles may not be 45°.)

2. Hold the square against the bottom edge for an outside corner and against the fold for an inside corner. The 45° position is placed at the point of cutting (Fig. 5-5). Mark the angle on the bottom leg.

3. Flip the square and mark the opposite angle from the same point.

4. Cut along angle lines with aviation snips.

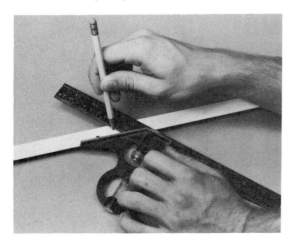

Fig. 5-5: *Marking the "V" cut.*

Installing Main Runners and Cross Tees

Before installing support components, mark their installation locations. Refer to the scale drawing or construction documents when determining main runner position. First, locate and mark the centerline of the room. Work out from the centerline and mark actual runner position on opposite walls. Normally these runners hang on 4' centers parallel to the long wall (Fig. 5-6).

Using Main Runner Reference Strings. Reference strings—sometimes called dry line, base line, or jet line—help position runners parallel to the centerline and guide trimming and interlocking. Place the strings on exact runner position marks set earlier. The strings must be hung at the level of hanger holes. They will be used not only to show main runner alignment, but also to bend hanger wire. Rest a main runner section on the wall molding flush against the wall. Line a hanger hole with the runner position mark and make a pencil mark through the hole (Fig. 5-7). Tie one end of the string to a nail and gently drive it behind the attached molding until the string and mark are even.

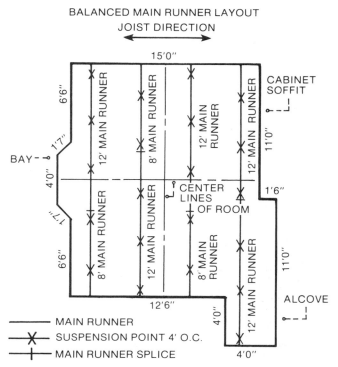

BALANCED MAIN RUNNER LAYOUT
JOIST DIRECTION

MAIN RUNNER
SUSPENSION POINT 4' O.C.
MAIN RUNNER SPLICE

Fig. 5-6: *Main runners are hung 4' O.C. parallel to the long wall.*

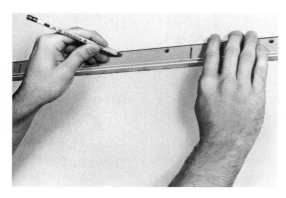

Fig. 5-7: Mark hanger hole level on the wall.

C-clamps or clamping pliers hold string in position and can be removed quickly. Figure 5-8 shows the proper method for clamping reference lines. Taut string is essential for correct positioning. When using Chicago Metallic wall molding, the string position is 1/4" above top molding edge; simply measuring 1" from the bottom of the molding yields correct string position. Hang one string for every main runner. (Check the holes in the runner that you are using.)

Cross Tee Reference String. The position of the first cross tee is marked by hanging a reference string across the main runner strings. Refer to your plans and measure from the centerline of the short wall to the cross tee position. Trimming and positioning of main runners depend upon the placement of cross tee strings (Fig. 5-9). Cross tee slot alignment depends upon this string forming true right angles with the main runners. The result of careless measurement will be panels that do not fit into the grid.

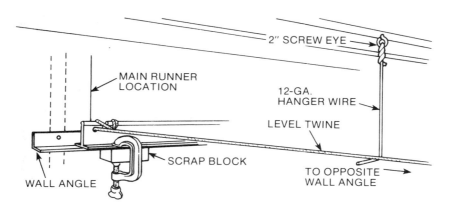

Fig. 5-8: Clamping the reference line in place.

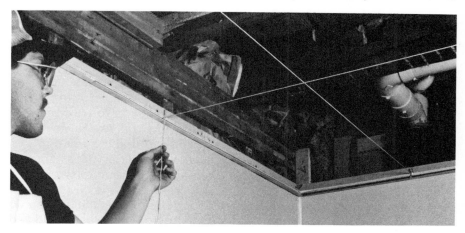

Fig. 5-9: *Accurate reference line placement is essential.*

Installing Hanger Wire. Hung from the original ceiling at 4' intervals above runner reference string, hanger wires are the primary support of such grid systems. Most residential and some light commercial structures incorporate wooden joint construction. Screw eyes, hooks, anchors, or sturdy nails are sunk into bottoms or sides of joists for hanger wire attachment (Fig 5-10). Whichever fastening technique is used, be absolutely sure of their strength and ability to support your ceiling. Whenever using screw threaded fasteners, drill 1/8" pilot holes to aid insertion; drawing threads across a bar of soap simplifies turning. Place the soaped fastener in the pilot hole, tap lightly with a hammer, and turn with pliers until solidly mounted in the joist.

Locate the first wire no more than 24" from the wall. Cut wires to a suitable length. Allow an extra 1' of wire over the amount of ceiling drop for wrapping; for instance, a ceiling dropped 1' requires 2' hanger wires.

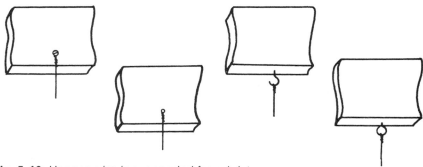

Fig. 5-10: *Hanger wire is suspended from joists.*

Insert a wire through the joist fastener and securely wrap it three times. The lower wire end should extend 6" below the reference string. Grasp the wire with a pliers where it strikes the string. Bend upward, pushing with your thumb, to a 105° angle (Fig. 5-11).

When joists are not exposed or out of line with runner position, you must attach fasteners in other manners. Nail 1" by 3" furring strips between joists to provide suitable attachment points for hanger wire when alignment is a problem. Treat the furring strips like joists; either insert screw fasteners or wrap the wire directly around the wood.

Locate concealed joists by thumping the cover material with a hammer. A hollow sounding thump indicates open areas between joists; a solid sound indicates joists. An electric or hand drill with a fine bit (1/8") can pinpoint exact joist location. Drill a row of holes across the suspected joist location. You will feel resistance when drilling into wood. Find two adjacent joists in the same fashion and measure the spacing between them; joist spacing is normally 16" or 24". Then measure the balance of joist positions.

Cutting or breaking out a portion of the old ceiling to determine joist spacing is quicker than drilling, but creates dust and dirt. Remove the covering across the room at right angles to the joists. Special fastening requirements are discussed in Chapter 6.

Sizing Main Runners. Accurate main runner sizing depends on precise cross tee reference string placement. Double-check the distance from the wall to the string before trimming main runners to length. The distance will match the drawings if correct. Whenever you measure, hold the rule edgewise to keep scale indications as close to the work as possible. When the line position is correct, trim the main runners.

The cross tee slots cut into the main runner *must align exactly* with the cross tee reference string. Base the trim position upon the measurement previously taken. Measure back from the end of the main runner to the next slot after the border distance. Then measure back from this slot the distance of the border, and make a mark.

For instance, in a sample installation, the cross tee reference string is 18" from the corner. Chicago Metallic main runner slots are spaced on 6" intervals with the first slot 3" from the end, which puts slots at 3", 9", 15", 21", and 27" on the runner. The slot that is 21" from the end is the slot immediately after the border measurement. The point that is 18" back from that slot (toward the component end) is marked and trimmed at that point. Once trimmed, a slot will be correctly positioned 18" from the wall.

Trimming Main Runners. The main runner lies on the full width of the lower molding leg. To preserve this condition, cut components in the following manner:

1. Cut the top flanges of the tee with an aviation snips.
2. Cut the stem (Fig. 5-12) to remove unwanted runner length. Proper

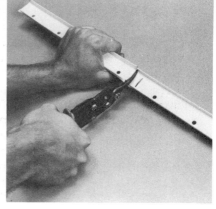

Fig. 5-11: *Bend the hanger wire where the reference line strikes it.*

Fig. 5-12: *Cutting the main runner to size.*

measuring and trimming techniques combine to provide consistent results and reduce overall installation time.

Hanging Main Runners. Your installation area now has wall molding in place and hanger wires bent. Your main runner board sections are cut and ready to be hung. Slip main runners onto the bent wire and check before securing (Fig. 5-13). Be sure to have hanger wires as close to vertical as possible because angled wire tends to pull the components out of level (Fig. 5-14).

Fig. 5-13: *Hang main runners from hanger wire.*

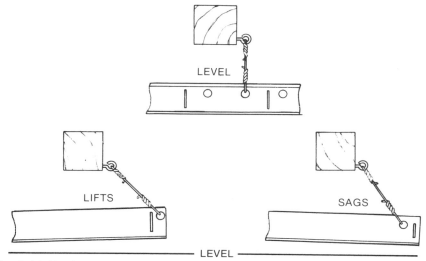

Fig. 5-14: *Vertical hanger wire reduces leveling problems.*

Place a carpenter's level on the main runner. When the component is true, secure the hanger wires with a minimum of three complete wraps (Fig. 5-15). Splice additional main runner sections to the first as needed; level and secure in the same manner. Continue hanging runners until all rows extend from wall to wall.

Splicing Runners. To knuckle joint splice the nondirectional main runners together, insert and bend the interconnecting tabs (one per side, Fig. 5-16). Hanging and splicing continues until the main runner rows are complete. Trim the last runner in each row for a snug fit against the wall.

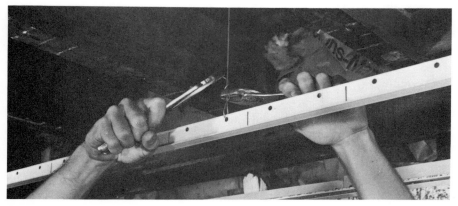

Fig. 5-15: *Secure main runners with three complete wraps.*

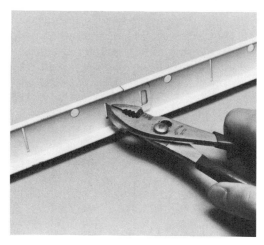

Fig. 5-16: *Knuckle joint splicing of a main runner.*

The installer is responsible for measuring from main runner marks to the cross tee reference string on every row. Individual measurement automatically adjusts to out-of-square rooms.

Scrap the trimmed off sections of the first and last main runner rows to reduce waste. Always place the trimmed end against the wall molding. To maintain proper support strength, avoid using trimmed pieces under 24″ long. Rooms under 12′ long receive the same treatment that large installations do. Halved main runners are easier to work with when aligning cross tee slots in small rooms. Splice the opposite ends together in the middle of the room to complete the rows.

Constantly check the level of components throughout this process. When disconnecting knuckle joint spliced runners, use a screwdriver (Fig. 5-17) or a pair of pliers.

Installing Cross Tees. When installing cross tees between the main runner and wall molding, make sure the first cross tee is directly below the

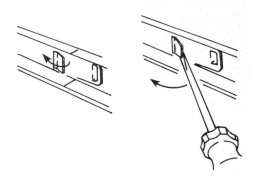

Fig. 5-17: *Spliced runner sections are separated easily when this knuckle joint is used to splice main runners.*

reference line. Measure between the main runner and wall molding to cut the border tees to width (Fig. 5-18). Tees are cut 1/8″ less than this figure for clearance. After cutting the cross tee, insert it between the main runner and molding with the factory-finished end to the main runner and the field cut end to the wall. Square the component intersection using a carpenter's square (Fig. 5-19).

Fig. 5-18: *Measure border tee width.*

Fig. 5-19: *Check installation with a carpenter's square.*

Following the installation procedure described in this section will ensure level cross tees; however, it never hurts to check with a carpenter's level. Remove cross tees by lifting up and pulling out of the slot, turning the tee slightly. Remember cross tees must be flush cut to rest on the lower leg of the wall molding, fitting snugly against the wall.

To prevent large areas of components from drifting out of line, some contractors pop-rivet every other component to the wall molding (Fig. 5-20). Never pop-rivet components unless you have checked their squareness. Follow the manufacturer's instructions for operating and fastening with a pop-rivet gun.

Your final main runner cross tee grid should look like the one shown in Fig. 5-21. All that remains is to place the panels.

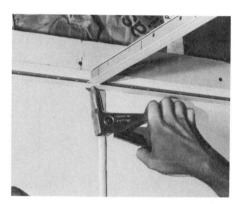

Fig. 5-20: *Pop-riveting components to wall molding reduces drifting.*

Fig. 5-21: *Completing the grid.*

Installing Ceiling Panels

Installing ceiling panels is the final phase of the installation procedure. Set ceiling panels into place after all grid installation has been completed.

Handling Ceiling Panels. When handling panels, be careful not to dirty the surface with fingerprints. Always pick them up by the edges to keep fingers and thumbs from touching the finished side. Wear gloves or use chalk, cornstarch, or talcum powder on hands before touching panels; this will greatly reduce the chance of marring panels with dirt or perspiration from hands.

Leave the completed ceiling in a clean, undamaged condition; always remove all trash. A soft brush or vacuum cleaner can clean loose dust from panel crevices. Brush only in one direction. Small marks and smudges disappear by using an art gum eraser (Fig. 5-22); wallpaper cleaner works on larger soiled areas. While paint, chalk, or pastels hide and fill small nicks, chips, or scrapes, typist's correction fluid or shoe polish can serve as white touch-up material. Always test each product on a scrap panel before using on installed panels.

Fig. 5-22: *An art gum eraser will remove minor smudges.*

Soiled acoustical ceiling panels can be washed with mild soapsuds, not detergent, but should never be soaked or immersed. A soft washcloth, soaked and wrung dry, is best for both light washing and clear-water rinsing.

Cutting Border Panels. Every border tile less than a whole panel must be cut and trimmed prior to installation. Cut each to the measurement between the wall and the component upright tee member. Cut the border 3/8" longer than the opening to account for the width of the bottom grid flanges. Do all cutting with the panels face up. Use either a sharp utility knife or fine-toothed hand saw. Always use a straightedge to guide your cuts; a square (Fig. 5-23) or scrap grid will also work well.

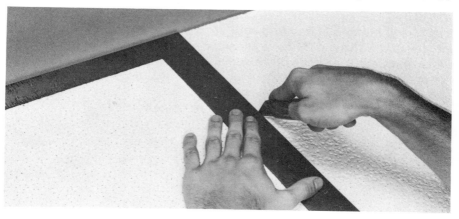

Fig. 5-23: *Cut panels using a square.*

Keep the knife blade sharp by occasionally using a honing stone as follows:

1. Place a few drops of light oil on the honing stone.
2. Hold blade against stone.
3. Press down on blade with fingers of free hand (Fig. 5-24).
4. Use light, even pressure, stroking blade against stone in a circular pattern.
5. After several strokes, turn knife over and repeat on other side. Before using the knife, be sure to remove all oil from the blade to avoid staining the panels.

Fig. 5-24: *Keep your knife blade sharp.*

If panels have a shadow line or revealed edge, the cut edge must be trimmed to match the revealed edge recess. To trim the edge, fit panels into the grid with the cut edge against the wall molding. Draw a line on the panel along the face edge of the wall molding. Make a face cut to match the depth of the recess; then, cut along the edge of the panel for proper depth (Fig. 5-25).

Fig. 5-25: Cutting a reveal edge.

Cut panel edges may be "feathered" (that is, lightly stroked) with a wood rasp to ensure a good fit in the grid system. To cut odd or curved panel shapes, use a coping saw, keyhole saw, or power saw. These and many other problem areas are dealt with in Chapter 6.

Placing Ceiling Panels. Ceiling panels drop into place by tilting them slightly, raising them above the level of the grid, and then lowering them onto the component flanges (Fig. 5-26). Be aware of the panel's texture and grain. Arrows are often printed on the back of each panel as an installation aid. You will be able to see an incorrectly placed panel

Fig. 5-26: Panels drop into the grid.

immediately. Other factors that may cause apparent variations in panel appearance include: texture and porosity of each panel, room lighting, and subjective differences between observers. To minimize the chance of production variation, use materials from the same production lot. The lot number is located on each carton of panels. Simulate occupancy lighting during installation to avoid shadow or hot spot problems. Periodically check color uniformity from floor level.

Install deeply-textured or fissured panels in one of these ways:

Uniform fissure direction—align arrows, usually found on backs of panels, in same direction;

Checkerboard—turn each successive panel 90°, and remember to alternate first panel of each row;

Random—install panels as grasped, truly nondirectional.

Chicago Metallic's 302 and 304 cross tees provide factory hold-down clips to reduce panel bounce and movement. After the panel has been placed, push the tab over the panel to secure it in positon. Hold-down clips are available for use with our Fire Front system.

Using a Progressive Installation. No matter how adept you are at planning, an occasional job requires installation with less than 3″ of clearance. When little space is available between the overhead and the new ceiling, complete the job progressively.

First, install molding and main runners as previously described. Then insert panels between the main runners before adding cross tees. Place a cross tee after each positioned panel and lock it into the main runners. The panel/tee alternation permits completion of a job with only enough clearance for eye hooks and wire.

Regardless of which installation method is used, a suspended ceiling significantly improves a room's appearance (Fig. 5-27).

Fig. 5-27: *A suspended ceiling grid will beautify any room.*

CONCEALED GRID CEILING SYSTEMS

Chicago Metallic produces additional ceiling grid accessories that are to be used for constructing a concealed ceiling system. With the addition of specific tees and splines, as well as special kerfed tiles (generally 12" by 12"), a monolithic ceiling can be accomplished. Contact your nearest Chicago Metallic office for details.

Chapter 6

SPECIAL CEILING INSTALLATIONS

Ideally, the installation of suspended ceilings would always take place in rooms that are square and that have no lighting, ductwork, windows, pipes, and/or stairwells. These conditions would ensure that the job would proceed smoothly and quickly. However, such conditions do not often occur. Careful planning of how obstructions are to be dealt with assures a quality finished job and allows installation to be practical and profitable.

GRID SYSTEM SOFFITS

In some instances, beams and ducts are located below the desired height of the ceiling. When this situation arises, it is necessary to box these structures in with a soffit (Fig. 6-1). Certain display room designs require that the ceiling be installed at two or three different levels connected by soffits (Fig. 6-2).

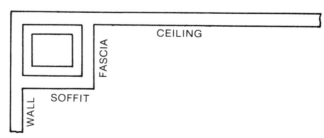

Fig. 6-1: *Soffits are used to cover obstructions below the ceiling level.*

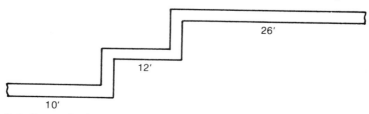

Fig. 6-2: *Some designs may employ several ceiling levels.*

Two types of exposed grid soffit systems can be constructed using Chicago Metallic ceiling components. All angles and pieces needed are available in precise, matching finishes. To ease the ordering process, a special product code has been developed. The basic suspended ceiling system has a number assigned to all components available for the particular grid design. A subcode, located as a suffix code, denotes finish type (Fig. 6-3). This provides for quick, foolproof ordering.

300-08

PRODUCT FINISH CODE

Fig. 6-3: Chicago Metallic's finish subcode simplifies ordering.

Before actual construction may begin, it is necessary to establish the lowest point of the object to be boxed in. Place bench marks on the wall adjacent to the soffit to be installed, if not already marked. Be sure these bench marks are at the same level as those at other corners. These marks will determine the specified height for the soffit's horizontal surface or for a lower ceiling level. Remember to add the height of the wall molding to this level (Fig. 6-4).

This adjusted ceiling level (height of soffit plus height of wall molding) should be marked at both ends of the wall adjacent to the soffit. Snap a chalk line at the level of these two marks (Fig. 6-5). The wall molding can now be installed. Align the top edge of the wall molding with the chalk line at all points.

From the wall, measure out the desired width of the soffit. This measurement should be marked on the upper level of the main runners. It indicates where to set the soffit's vertical section. A chalk line, aligned

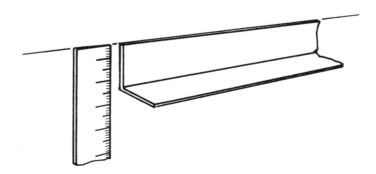

Fig. 6-4: Remember to add molding height to all ceiling level measurements.

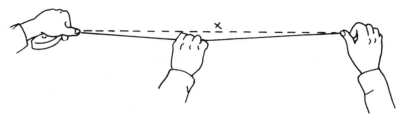

Fig. 6-5: *Snapping a chalk line.*

with the marks just located, is now snapped against the main runners. This line is the guide for installing the U-shaped molding which holds the vertical section of the soffit in place. Let main runners extend approximately 1' beyond the point where the soffit's vertical drop begins.

Main runners or cross tees to box in the soffit area can now be installed. *Note:* If the total length of the soffit's vertical and horizontal sections is less than 4', cross tees may be used to box in the soffit. If the total length is greater than 4', main runners must be utilized. Before installing each runner, measure the vertical length onto the runner.

Installation Method A

If upper and lower ceiling levels must be centered independently or the module must change from level to level, the method shown in Fig. 6-6 is used. If such considerations are of no concern, a mechanical soffit (Fig. 6-7) may be used. Both soffits employ the same basic construction techniques.

The two soffits have lower corners formed by cutting the bulbs and webs of the suspension components. Figure 6-8D and E illustrate the two cuts necessary to form the proper soffit angles. After cutting, the flange faces should be bent to a 90° angle. These bends must be reinforced to provide adequate grid stability. This is done with flat metal angles or corner caps. These reinforcements may be pop-riveted to the runners for maximum rigidity. Large drops in ceiling height will require 45° bracing via rigid members.

A wall angle is pop-riveted to the lower corner. This not only provides a neat appearance, but also supports the horizontal panels. The top corner varies between the two methods. In Fig. 6-6, the wall angle is placed with one side visible. To do this, pop-rivet the angle to the vertical component section and the upper level suspension component. Notice that the vertical suspension component is separated from the upper level component by cutting the web and flanges completely. The angle pop-riveted to the top establishes the proper 90° bend.

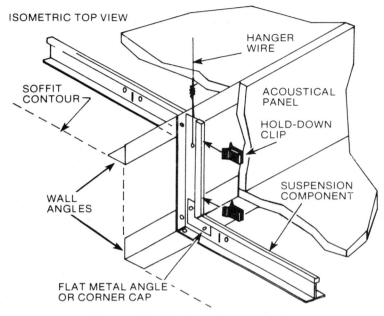

ISOMETRIC TOP VIEW

HANGER WIRE

SOFFIT CONTOUR

ACOUSTICAL PANEL

HOLD-DOWN CLIP

WALL ANGLES

SUSPENSION COMPONENT

FLAT METAL ANGLE OR CORNER CAP

Fig. 6-6: *Exposed soffit permitting independent centering.*

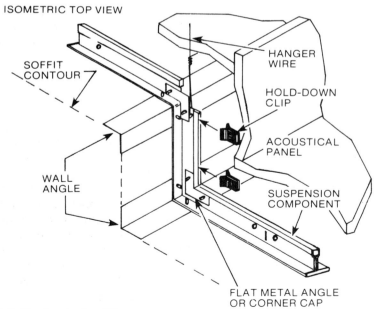

ISOMETRIC TOP VIEW

SOFFIT CONTOUR

HANGER WIRE

HOLD-DOWN CLIP

ACOUSTICAL PANEL

WALL ANGLE

SUSPENSION COMPONENT

FLAT METAL ANGLE OR CORNER CAP

Fig. 6-7: *Mechanical soffit.*

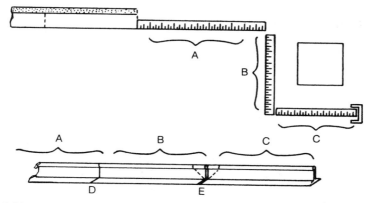

Fig. 6-8: *Measure (A) the distance from the previously installed main runner, and measure the (B) vertical and (C) horizontal soffit sections. Two cuts required for the mechanical soffit are the (D) straight cut and (E) "V" cut.*

The mechanical soffit's top angle has two faces showing when properly installed. The top corner is made by cutting the web and bulb only. Bending at this cut produces a 90° angle while the flanges remain attached. This bend is covered by the wall angle as it is pop-riveted to the upper level suspension components and the vertical runner.

In order to preserve the correct grid dimensions, horizontal panels should be placed in first. Vertical panels are rested in place and secured with hold-down clips. Such installation will prevent ceiling breathing and preserve the acoustical qualities of the ceiling. Attach a hanger wire to each vertical component section as illustrated. This will ensure stability and proper ceiling alignment.

Installation Method B

This method uses the main runners as both vertical and horizontal supports. The soffit is completed as part of a continuous runner system. Refer to Fig. 6-7 for the steps concerning the construction of a soffit via Method B. The procedure outlined for Method A should be duplicated up to the point where the wall molding is attached. Before continuing, make sure the main runners are installed and the soffit wall molding is attached.

Measure and mark the distance from the previously installed runner to where the vertical face of the soffit will be located. Remember to leave sufficient space between the grid and the object being boxed in. Not only will the precaution ease the insertion of the tile, but it will provide air space insulation within the soffit. Check the manufacturer's requirements for tile placement, especially if the object being boxed in transfers heated air or water or if the covered object requires ventilation.

Measure the vertical and horizontal faces of the soffit (Fig. 6-8A, B, and C) and mark these locations on the runner. Check these measurements carefully because they determine the proper soffit configuration.

Having marked these two points, make the cuts on the main runners (Fig. 6-8D and E). A straight cut is made in the main runner web at the mark designating the beginning of the vertical section of the soffit. The mark where the horizontal portion is to begin receives a 90° "V" cut. This allows the runner to be bent easily without buckling. The lower horizontal portion of the main runner should be trimmed 1/4" shy of the measured distance to permit proper seating in the wall molding. Now bend and hang the main runner. Since such cutting and bending reduce the strength of the main runner, attach hanger wires (1) near the break in the upper ceiling portion of the runner and (2) near the junction of the vertical and lower ceiling sections of the runner.

The end of the runner should rest on the lower level wall molding. Install the upper ceiling panels first up to the point where the soffit begins; then, install pieces of "L" molding between runners for proper trim. The junctions of both the horizontal and vertical portions of the soffit should receive this treatment.

Place vertical panels in the soffit first. Hold-down clips are recommended to keep the panels in an upright position. Installation of horizontal panels in the lower ceiling level completes the procedure.

INSTALLATION OF GRID AROUND COLUMNS AND POSTS

When a column is located in a room where a grid ceiling is to be installed, proper planning will prevent unnecessary complications. Accurate measurement of the column hole location will aid in establishing a ceiling pattern. To scribe a circle on a ceiling panel:

1. Measure the diameter of the column. Divide the diameter by two in order to get the radius.

2. Set the scribe points at this radius measure on your rule. When properly spaced, lock the thumbscrew.

3. Set one leg of the scribe at the center around which the circle is to be drawn. Use the other leg to draw the circle (Fig. 6-9).

It is important to lay out the suspended ceiling components so that the main runners and cross tees miss the column.

Once the column size has been determined, a corresponding hole may be cut in the panel. If the panel is glass fiber, vinyl-faced, or foam, the shortest possible cut may be made between the cutout and the nearest edge of the panel. The characteristics of these materials allow the panels

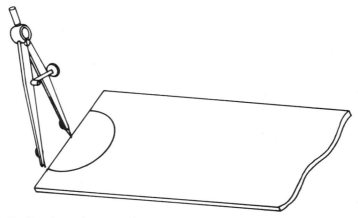

Fig. 6-9: *Scribe the column radius onto the tile.*

to flex without breaking. They may be tilted or splayed into place around the column (Fig. 6-10).

If the panels being installed are made from heavier or stiffer materials, the method described will not work. Instead, cut the hole with a fine-toothed keyhole saw or utility knife, according to the dimension and location of the column. Bisect the panel on a line which runs through the center of the hole (Fig. 6-11). Install the two pieces around the column. To

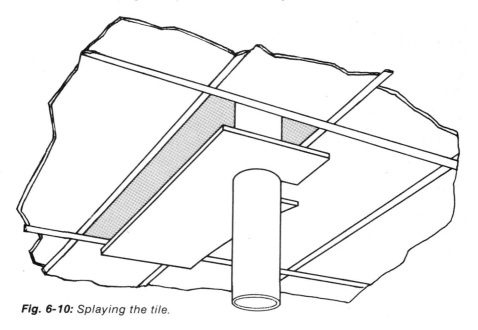

Fig. 6-10: *Splaying the tile.*

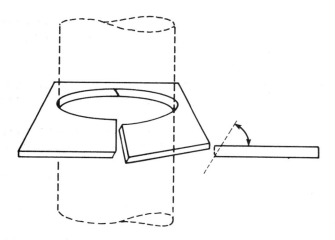

Fig. 6-11: *Stiff ceiling panels are bisected.*

ensure a proper fit and no movement, a bisected tile must be re-fastened by gluing two pieces of tile over the bisected cut (Fig. 6-12).

When a column or post is located in a room where grid ceiling is to be installed, the ceiling pattern should be so planned that the main runners and cross tees miss the column. One exception: If the column is quite large, attach wall molding to it at correct ceiling height. Be sure to put bench marks on the column to accurately place wall molding in position.

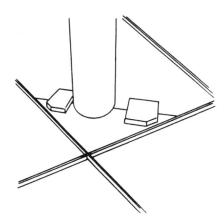

Fig. 6-12: *Glue scrap pieces of tile over the joint to ensure alignment.*

With smaller columns or posts, proceed in the following manner:

1. Install main runners and cross tees in the area around the column in the normal manner (Fig. 6-13).

2. Cut two cross tees to 23-3/4" length.

3. Lay these short cross tees parallel to the main runners and adjacent to the column. Rest the ends of these cross tees on the flanges of the regular cross tees.

4. First measure the distance from the regular cross tees to the center of the post. Then measure the distance between the two short cross tees (23-3/4" length units).

5. Cut two panels to fit between these two tees and between the column and two regular runners.

6. Butt these two pieces of panel together on the floor; transfer measurements to them for placement of the column.

7. Scribe and cut the circle in the panels for the column. Lay the panels into position between the cross tees. The panels should be flush around the column.

8. Measure, cut, and install panels to fit the areas between the two main runners and the parallel cross tees.

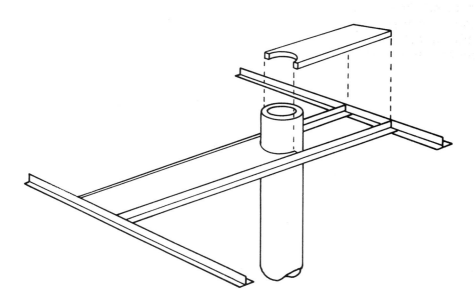

Fig. 6-13: *Boxing-in small columns.*

STAIRWELL INSTALLATION

A suspended ceiling is easily installed in most home stairwells. The width and sloping angle of many stairwells makes fabrication slightly different from regular room applications. Most stairwells are less than 4' wide, eliminating the need for main runners.

The first step in construction involves the proper installation of wall molding. Because this molding provides all support for the ceiling, it is important that care be taken when it is hung. Molding position should be leveled and marked on the two short parallel walls. These marks will establish the angle of the ceiling. Place the ends of a chalk line at the adjacent corners of opposite short walls. The line itself should be taut against the long wall and snapped. Repeat this procedure for the other long wall. Wall angles may now be applied along these chalk lines.

Once the wall angles have been attached, install the ceiling panels. Trim the panels to the proper dimensions. Starting at the lowest point, place the first panel. This panel will be supported on three sides by wall angle. Trim a cross tee to fit between and rest firmly on the sloping wall angle. Slide the tee under the panel to support the fourth side. Make sure the tee abuts the ceiling panel. Place successive panels and tees until the ceiling is complete. This installation technique is known as packing the panels and tees. *Note:* Use this method only when the span between moldings is less than 4'; no main runners are needed as the ceiling weight can easily be supported by the wall angles.

Boxing Window Tops and Stairwells

In certain installations, the customer may wish to lower the ceiling beneath a window top or stairwell. Basement installations are a good example of this. If a window or stairwell extends above the height of the new ceiling, it must be boxed in. Construct a valence or frame made of 3/4" finished lumber to fit from ceiling level to the top of the window or stairwell. Proper dimensions are important when planning the valence size. It should be wide enough to accept the bulk of open draperies and deep enough to allow the window to be opened (Fig. 6-14).

To construct the valence, first measure the area to be boxed in. Mark these measurements on the existing ceiling or joists. Line the edge of a 2 by 4 properly against these marks and nail to the joists. Cut and screw planks of the desired width to these boards. A board measured and cut to proper dimensions should be installed onto the 2 by 4s to cover the broad exposed face.

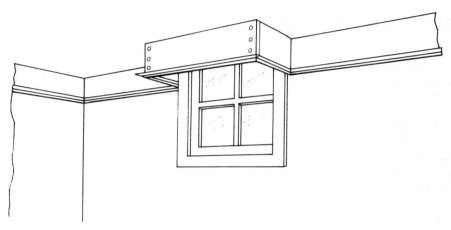

Fig. 6-14: *Window valence.*

The entire valence should be finished in a manner that is suitable to both the ceiling and room design. Keep in mind that only the inside surfaces of the boxed area and the lower edges will be exposed. After the unit is finished, attach wall molding to the lower edge of the wood frame valence.

In remodeling work, high windows can also be accommodated by building a frame from wall molding sections to hold the panel in, forming a vertical box (Fig. 6-15). Attach the wall molding to the old ceiling with molly-type or toggle fasteners. Then pop-rivet the two angles together where necessary to hold the panels.

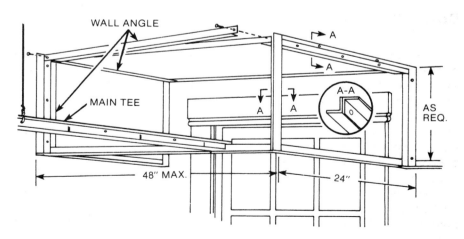

Fig. 6-15: *Construction technique for a grid frame.*

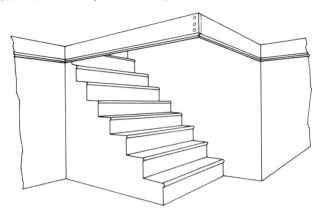

Fig. 6-16: *A stairwell valence.*

For most stairwells with a lowered ceiling, a small wall frame valence must be built to fit the stairwell opening. The procedure is the same as outlined for boxing in a window. Installations such as these are not regularly encountered. Because of their unique nature, the situation should be carefully analyzed and the valence construction planned according to individual requirements (Fig. 6-16).

ATTACHING PARTITIONS TO EXPOSED GRID SYSTEMS

Demountable partitions often need to be attached to suspended ceilings. Besides providing a stable point of connection, the regular spacing of suspension components creates a useful module for the planning of office spacing. Figure 6-17 shows a method of attaching Chicago Metallic Corporation demountable gypsum partitions to a CMC exposed ceiling. This method will also work for other manufacturers' gypsum panel/stud partitions and studless laminated partitions of gypsum or steel construction. Use foam tape or caulking at the interface of the suspended ceiling and the top partition track to serve as a light and sound barrier.

The ceiling track is centered below the exposed component and attached through the component web with self-tapping screws. The drywall track is then centered in the ceiling track and screwed through it into the component web. The studs are inserted into the drywall track and attached to it by crimping, punching, and pop-riveting or using self-tapping screws. Gypsum panels are then placed into the ceiling track and attached to studs with proper fasteners. Studless laminated panels are inserted directly into a compatible width ceiling track and attached with proper fasteners.

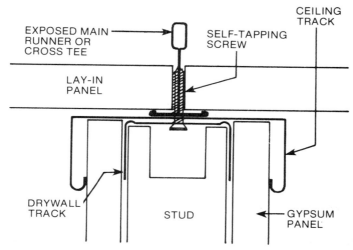

Fig. 6-17: *Attaching partitions directly to grid.*

VENT INSTALLATIONS

If the level of the new ceiling is to be below that of the existing ventilation system (heating or air conditioning), the ducted vents must be extended to the new ceiling height and a grille attached. The easiest way to extend a ceiling duct opening is to have a metal sleeve made to fit between the old opening and the new ceiling height. Fasten it to the original opening and to the grille (Fig. 6-18). Of course, all ductwork must comply with local building and heating code guidelines. If vents are used to transport heated air, temperatures that may safely be used with the specific panel should also be considered.

The main concern relating to the suspended ceiling system is that no weight be placed upon the panels. All ducting must be suspended independently of the ceiling grid. Again, this will ensure that the proper conditions are maintained for which the grid was designed, as well as adding to the dependability and long life of the suspended ceiling. Caution should be exercised when lightweight ceiling panels are installed against any duct carrying furnace heat. If this is the case, either the panels should not be installed as close to the ductwork as possible or a special thermal barrier should be placed between the duct and the ceiling panel.

Select vent grilles compatible with the ceiling panel the customer has chosen. Check to make sure that the vent grille color is one that matches or blends with the suspended ceiling system finish. Make panel installation around the grille by accurately measuring and cutting the vent open-

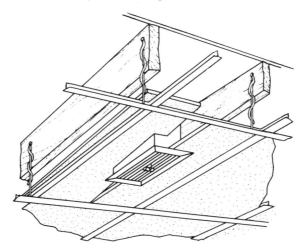

Fig. 6-18: *A metal sleeve extends the vent opening to the ceiling level.*

ing in the panel and bisecting it down the middle. The two panel sections can then be inserted into the grid system.

To frame out exposed ducts or pipes, use a wooden frame to hold the vertical panels. You can also build a frame using wall moldings. To form a corner with wall moldings, cut one flange of the molding and bend it so that the cut edges overlap. Make short diagonal cuts in the flange that will be covered, slip the cut-to-size panel in place, and bend the joints to hold it in place (Fig. 6-19).

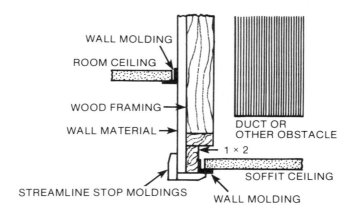

Fig. 6-19: *A wooden frame method of covering ductwork.*

Chapter 7

OTHER CEILING CONSIDERATIONS

A contractor must have a working knowledge of available ceiling accessories to completely meet customer needs and achieve maximum project profitability. Optional features will often sell ceilings if alternate installation methods are unavailable or too costly. The plenum above the suspended grid provides easy access for hidden component servicing. Storage areas, ventilation systems, heating panels, audio speakers, and lighting systems are just some of the extras which make suspended grid more than just a ceiling; have customers consider all the options.

LIGHTING INSTALLATION

Lights are the most familiar of all ceiling accessories. Proper installation techniques prevent grid damage and ensure safety. Grid is designed to support ceiling tile. All additional loads require extra hanger wire support.

Electrical conduit, wire, fixture boxes, terminals, and all other related installations are completed by an electrician before lights are installed. Electrical connection points help locate the proper grid for lighting placement. Remember to hang fixtures from screw eyes with hanger wire; never rest fixtures directly on the grid flanges. Be aware of fixture height requirements (Fig. 7-1).

Surface Mounted Lighting

Support surface mounted light fixtures and lightweight items with a wood attachment block suspended from above. Measure the exact distance between the webs or stems of main runners or tees and cut a 2 by 4 to this length. Lay the wood section on top of the panel, and secure by running two 2" screws *through* the web or stem of the grid member and into the wood ends (Fig. 7-2A). This provides solid material that is able to receive attachment fasteners for surface mounted lights or track sup-

71

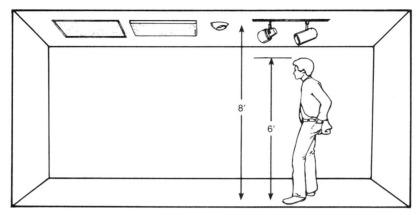

Fig. 7-1: *Lighting should never interfere with movement in the room.*

ports. *Note:* Add extra hanger wire to the grid where attached to the wood section. This helps carry any extra load on the grid system.

Lay-In Light Fixtures

Of all fixture types, lay-in requires the most straightforward installation. Their dimensions are slightly less than standard grid openings (2' by 2' and 2' by 4') and are easily lowered in from above. The grid flange alone will not support fixture weight; always hang with a minimum of four hanger wires (one per corner).

Incandescent Lighting

Incandescent lights, even in reflective high hat or can fixtures, are too hot for plastic panels. Install such fixtures on a subframe because they are generally smaller than grid openings. As before, extra hanger wire supports the components at subframe attachment points.

Ceiling specialists recommend securely affixing the canister to a pair of molding sections long enough to rest on main runner flanges (Fig. 7-2B). The alternative is an independently hung fixture. Cut an appropriate fixture opening in the panel and finish with a trim ring or grille. Never use incandescent lights in fire rated applications.

Note: No matter what type of lighting fixture is used, all manufacturer's requirements must be met. Both lighting and ceiling components are designed with certain circumstances in mind; these conditions must be compatible.

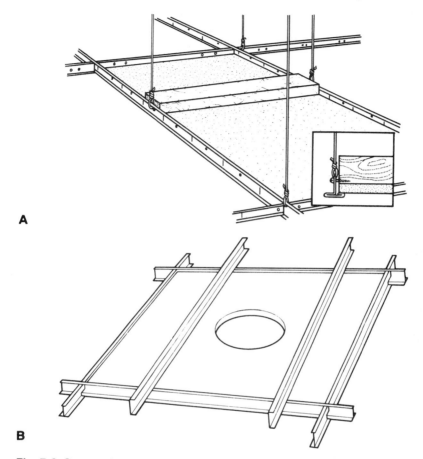

A

B

Fig. 7-2: *Supporting structures for (A) surface mounted lighting and (B) canister fixtures.*

Astralite ceiling light panels from Chicago Metallic (Fig. 7-3) are a simple, handsome method of integrating an incandescent lighting system into a suspended ceiling. Available in ceiling light panels or solid decorator panels, these 2' by 2' steel panels are coated in either brass, chrome, white, architectural bronze, or sandstone to lend a variety of accents to any decor.

Astralites weigh only 8-1/2 pounds and are easy to install. Simply remove the back of the unit's junction box and make appropriate connections with the electrical supply lines in the ceiling. For 2' by 4' ceiling layouts, an extra 2' cross tee must be added to the grid to accommodate panel size. Astralites should be equipped with 75 watt conventional (tear-shaped) lamps or R-40 reflector type lamps up to 150 watts.

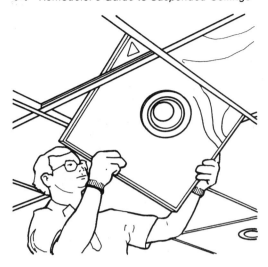

Fig. 7-3: Astralite panels house a lighting fixture and are easy to install.

Surface Mounted Track Lights

Avoid attaching track lights directly to grid members. This arrangement is not impossible, but Chicago Metallic does not recommend it. If you do install tracks, follow the procedures described for surface mounted fixtures.

CEILING HEAT PANELS

One of the newest options for suspended ceilings is the radiant heat panel. Such installations are meant for supplementary heating purposes only. Radiant heat warms objects, not the air. Panels are electrically operated and usually come pre-wired.

Install these panels (Fig. 7-4) similarly to lay-in lighting fixtures. The 2' by 4' elements are placed in the grid, resting on component flanges. Additional support mechanics vary according to manufacturer's provisions. As with anything other than a lightweight ceiling panel, use additional hanger wires to make certain the grid is not damaged.

The panel should be wired by an electrician to an outlet box above the panel. Connect a standard ON/OFF switch or install specially designed thermostat controls. The controls permit optimum regulation of panel heat.

These heating elements are excellent sources of supplementary heat where other heating elements are too dangerous or difficult to install. Various manufacturers claim that these panels may reduce the tempera-

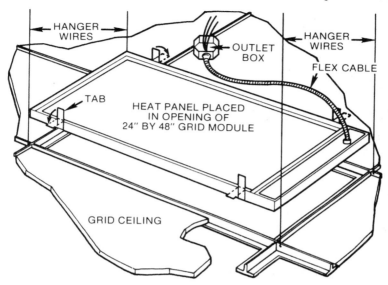

Fig. 7-4: *Ceiling heat panels are laid in place like tile.*

ture of the main heating supply by 5° to 8° with no significant comfort effect (depending on personal comfort requirements).

Several manufacturers of ceiling heat panels are: Airtex Corporation, 2900 North Western Avenue, Chicago, Illinois 60618; Federal Pacific Electric Group, 150 Avenue L, Newark, New Jersey 07101; Aztech International, Ltd., 2417 Aztech Road, N.E. Albuquerque, New Mexico 87107; Emerson Electric Co., Special Products Division, 5655 Campus Parkway, Hazelwood, Missouri 63042.

BEAMS FOR A SUSPENDED CEILING

Your customer may wish to add decorative charm to a suspended ceiling with wood-look beams (Fig. 7-5). There are several types of vinyl wood-grained beams, but the basic installation procedure for a *typical* beam is as follows:

1. Attach two of the provided hangers 6" from each end of the main beams. Fasten the beams to the main runners (or to cross tees) by using pliers to bend the hanger tabs on each beam over the T-flange (Fig. 7-6).

2. Space the other hangers provided with each beam at equal distances between the end hangers at each beam. If cross beams are used, space hangers close to the cross beam locations to obtain a tight joint between beams.

Fig. 7-5: *Wood-look beams provide a unique appearance for the ceiling.*

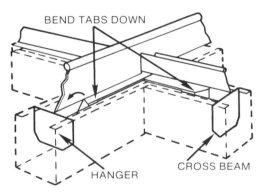

Fig. 7-6: *Bend hanger tabs over the T-flange.*

3. Arrange the beams by spreading the top sections so the flange can be inserted on top of the hangers. Apply firm pressure inward along the upper edge of each beam, locking it into position (Fig. 7-7). It may be necessary to cut off a portion of the beam flange at the end to fit under the wall angle.

Most beams of this type are 12' in length. When the beam must be cut to a length less than 12', use a metal hacksaw or aviation snips. Cut the beam slightly shorter than the ceiling width (about 1/8" shorter is suggested), to allow the beam to be turned and fitted between the walls. If a beam longer than 12' is needed, join all or part of two 12' beams. The last section of the beam to span the room should be cut as close as possible to reduce the

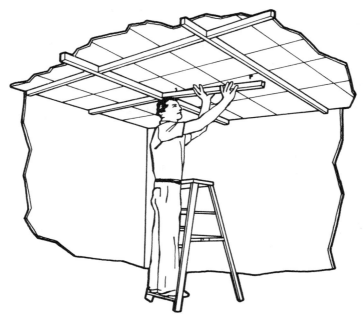

Fig. 7-7: *Firm pressure locks beams into place.*

clearance at the wall. Space hangers about 2″ on each side of the joint. Snap the first beam in place. As shown in Fig. 7-8, apply a wood block, fitting the end to hold the beam straight. Tightly snap the second beam in place against the first beam.

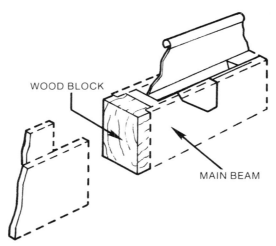

WOOD BLOCK

MAIN BEAM

Fig. 7-8: *A wood block aligns beam joints.*

When installing 4' cross beams between main beams, locate hangers about 2" from each end of the cross beam. The depth of the 4' beam is slightly less than the depth of the 12' beam, so metal ends will not be seen when the cross beam is installed against the side of the long beam. Do not use a 4' beam to lengthen a 12' beam; the two beams will not match in height.

There are a variety of beam sections in addition to the one described. For further information, check with your lumberyard or home center.

AUDIO SPEAKER INSTALLATION

The flush mounted audio system is another ceiling option frequently requested by customers. Good sound distribution, hidden speaker wires, and increased floor space otherwise taken by speaker cabinets make above-grid audio installations attractive.

To begin installation, determine speaker location. Remove the panel that will conceal the speaker. Cut a hole slightly smaller than the speaker grille and attach the grille to the panel with appropriate fasteners. Paint the grille to match the panel where an integrated look is required. Complete all finishing work prior to installation.

Support the speaker's weight with additional hanger wire. Cut a pair of 2 by 4s to fit between the main runners of the suspended grid. Temporarily place the boards into the grid so they rest on flanges; the fit must be snug, yet it cannot misalign the grid. After checking the fit, remove the boards.

Next, place the panel, with the grille installed, on the floor and place the speaker on top of the grille. Lay the 2 by 4s beside the speakers and mark the screw hole locations. Mount the speakers with 2 by 4s on the speaker lip side opposite the grille. Insert the panel into the grid, gently lowering

Fig. 7-9: *Run screws through the main runner into board ends.*

the speaker unit onto the grid. Run screws through the main runner into the ends of the supporting boards (Fig. 7-9). Make sure enough additional hanger wires have been attached to support the heavier load. Make all necessary audio connections above the ceiling, and replace the remaining ceiling panels.

EXHAUST FAN INSTALLATION

A finished attic may become overheated during summer months if some sort of exhaust system is not provided to remove trapped, heated air. A large exhaust fan creates air movement and promotes cooling throughout the entire house, removing heat and moisture.

Prior to installation, unpack the fan and make sure you have all mounting hardware. Next, make an opening for the fan. If the suspended ceiling has already been installed, remove the ceiling panels from the desired placement area. You must remove the floor joist running through the installation opening. Nail a 2 by 4 to the joist behind the cut locations to act as a temporary brace (Fig. 7-10). Using a carpenter's square, mark the cut. This measurement must equal the width of the fan plus the header to be installed. Carefully cut away the floor joist (Fig. 7-11).

Fig. 7-10: *The braced joist is marked for cutting.*

After removing the cross tee, nail the header to the exposed joist end and both adjacent joists (Fig. 7-12). You may remove the temporary brace. The header just installed yields the exact width dimension of the fan; the existing joists are probably not spaced to the correct dimension of the fan. Measure the length for a board which will extend the joist to adjust the opening size (Fig. 7-13). Nail this header to the previously installed header and the supporting member at the opposite end (Fig. 7-14).

Fig. 7-11: *Cutting the floor joist.*

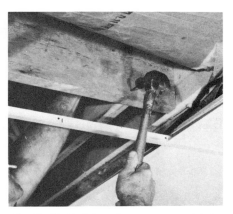

Fig. 7-12: *Nail header to exposed joist.*

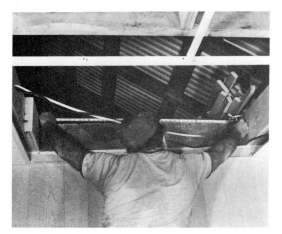

Fig. 7-13: *Measuring opening size.*

Fig. 7-14: *Nailing adjacent header.*

Make a framework that is slightly smaller than the actual fan (Fig. 7-15) to provide support and a weather seal when the fan is in place. Attach the assembled frame to the boxed-out area. Then apply the weather seal to the edge of the fan housing, securing the rubber strip with tape to prevent shifting during installation (Fig. 7-16).

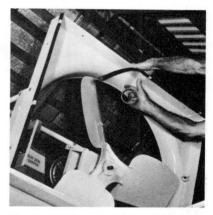

Fig. 7-15: *The framework provides a weather seal.*

Fig. 7-16: *Tape the rubber seal to the fan body.*

Next, place and center the fan on the frame. Nail small wood blocks against each side of the fan to secure and prevent it from shifting (Fig. 7-17). Remove the electrical box cover to facilitate power hookup (Fig. 7-18). *Always turn off the power at its source when making electrical connections.* Pull a circuit breaker or fuse; simply turning a switch off may not provide adequate protection. Screw wire nuts securely onto wire splices to ensure safe connection. Once all connections are complete,

Fig. 7-17: *Nail wood blocks to hold fan position.*

Fig. 7-18: Removing the electrical box cover facilitates power hookup.

Fig. 7-19: Adjust belt tension.

Fig. 7-20: The louvered fan covering.

double-check work against manufacturer's instructions and replace the cover plate. Adjust the belt tension and tighten the bolts that slide the motor on the mounting rails (Fig. 7-19). Put insulation around the edge of the fan for a positive weather seal.

The final operation involves placing the louvered vent (Fig. 7-20) below the fan. Lift the vent plate into place and mark the locations of the screw holes. Drill into the main runner (Fig. 7-21) and insert metal screws. Finally, cut a panel to fit any small openings and lay the pieces into the grid (Fig. 7-22).

The finished fan opens the louvers when turned on. When the fan is turned off, the louvers provide a positive seal against downdrafts.

Fig. 7-21: *Screw the louver to the grid.*

Fig. 7-22: *Fit ceiling panel around completed installation.*

CEILING FAN INSTALLATION

The ceiling fan is probably the most popular ceiling accessory available today. It has a classic look and is of practical benefit to home heating and cooling. The fan cannot, however, be hung directly from the suspended grid because the hanger wire cannot support the weight of the motor unit. The fan must be hung from the original ceiling joists. Two methods of hanging ceiling fans are discussed in the following paragraphs. Both methods use the ceiling joist as the main support because it provides the 50 pounds of support that the fan needs.

The first method uses extended hanger pipe. The additional pipe lowers the fan motor housing to an acceptable level. When you have selected the desired location, make sure the installed fan blades will be at least 18" from the nearest wall. To avoid any possible danger, hang the fan no lower than 7' from the floor. To determine how much additional hanger pipe is needed, add the desired height above the floor (D) and the dimension of the fan from the lowest point of the blade hub to the hanger stem (F) (Fig. 7-23). Subtract this figure from the height (H). (Measure the height from the floor to the bottom of the joist.) The result (X) is the length of additional hanger pipe. The calculation for Fig. 7-23 looks like this:

$$H - (D + F) = X$$
$$11' - (7' + 1') = 3' \text{ hanger pipe}$$

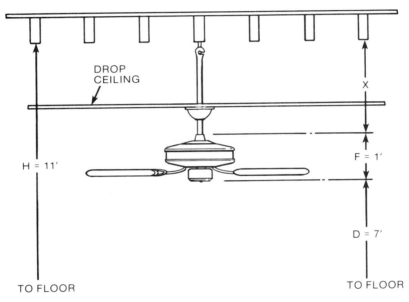

Fig. 7-23: *Using a hanger pole extension.*

Hanger pipe is available through the ceiling fan manufacturer. Standard lengths of 36" pipe can be cut to the proper length and are easily joined using pole couplers. If hanger pipe is not available, use 1/2" diameter pipe such as conduit or black iron. This pipe must be threaded to screw into the motor fan housing.

Follow the instructions provided with the ceiling fan for proper installation. Cut a hole the diameter of the pipe in the ceiling panel, directly below the location of the hook which will support the fan. Insert the pipe through the hole and hang the fan. The canopy should be placed between the fan motor housing and the ceiling panel. Secure the canopy to the pipe with the setscrew to give the illusion that the fan is attached to the suspended ceiling.

The second method of ceiling fan support involves lowering the actual attachment point. Locate the joist above the desired installation point. This joist will be the supporting member on which the extender is constructed. To determine how long the extension boards must be, add the desired height (D) to the total length of the fan unit (U) (Fig. 7-24). This length (U) is measured from the point of attachment to the lowest part of the fan. Subtract the total placement height (D + U) from the height (H). (The height is measured from the floor to the top of the joist.) The result (X) is the length of board necessary to sufficiently lower the fan attachment point.

This calculation, done for Fig. 7-24, appears as follows:

$$H - (D + U) = X$$
$$12' - (7' + 2.5') = 2.5' \text{ of board}$$

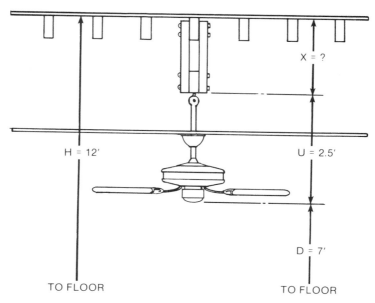

Fig. 7-24: *"Lowering" the joist for ceiling mounting.*

Cut 2 by 4s to the length just figured and place them on either side of the ceiling joist, one end flush against the ceiling boards and the broad side against the joists. Run two bolts through both boards and the ceiling joist. To ensure stability of the lower attachment point, place the bolts one above the other.

Bolt a block of wood with the same dimensions as the joist to the other end of the lowering boards. This block will be the mounting area for the ceiling fan. Follow the manufacturer's instructions to complete the installation. Whenever the instructions refer to the joist, perform the installation technique on the lowered wood block. Remember to use the setscrew to affix the canopy below the ceiling panel.

PLANT TRAPEZE INSTALLATION

Hanging plants are another popular decorating feature currently incorporated in homes. Homeowners with newly installed suspended ceilings may be tempted to hang plants directly from the gridwork. This practice should be discouraged. The suspended ceiling system is designed to support the weight of ceiling panels and limited extra insulation. Hanging plants from the grid may adversely affect the ceiling's performance.

An adequate support system for hanging plants can, however, easily be provided. All loads to be hung at or around the suspended ceiling level should receive their support from the original ceiling. First locate the joists directly above the desired location. Mark these locations and insert large eye screws. Temporarily hang a length of chain from each eye hook with an S-hook, cutting the chain to the proper length.

Cut holes into the ceiling panel to accommodate the chain. Cut a piece of doweling as long as the space between the chains. Before permanently installing the trapeze, paint the exposed chain and dowel the same color as the ceiling. After painting, secure the supporting chain by closing the

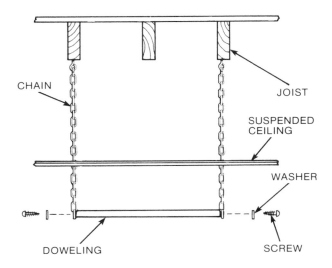

CHAIN

JOIST

SUSPENDED
CEILING

WASHER

DOWELING

SCREW

Fig. 7-25: The plant trapeze.

S-hooks through the eye hooks. Fasten the dowel to the chains with screws and washers (Fig. 7-25). The finished trapeze should hang 1" to 2" below the ceiling level to facilitate easy hanging of plant baskets.

INSULATION

The natural insulating qualities of suspended ceilings are an added bonus to the consumer. Whether the installation of the new ceiling is for practical, cosmetic, or aesthetic purposes, the nature of the system's design helps to effectively insulate an area. More efficient use of energy is the result.

A suspended ceiling reduces the volume of air within a room as well as ceiling height. As the distance between the floor and ceiling decreases, efficiency increases; this provides a very desirable heating situation. A decreased area to heat allows the heating units to operate for shorter periods of time at reduced levels, passing on additional savings in the form of extended unit life. Rising warm air is kept closer to the actual living area with a suspended ceiling system.

Install a vapor barrier to ensure that the rising warm air will not easily penetrate the suspended level. This combined with tight-fitting flanges and panels creates a tight seal that will not allow heated air to rapidly leak into the outer atmosphere. In the summer, the ceiling panels keep cool air in the room and retain sun-heated air in the plenum.

Highlight these points while discussing possible suspended ceiling installations with customers. If normal insulation installation techniques are not possible, inform them that Chicago Metallic's systems can be further insulated. Depending on the type of panel selected, an additional one-half pound per square foot of evenly distributed insulation may be added. This extra insulation can drastically improve a room's energy efficiency.

Other possible ceiling installations involve insulation contracts as the primary job. An attic or similar room may have batting type insulation stapled to the old roof surface overhead. If the customer desires to use the area for living purposes, suggest a suspended ceiling system. Always acquaint prospective customers with possibilities like this. It is an excellent chance to maximize the customer's benefit from his investment while increasing sales.

R-Value

The purpose of insulation is to seal off the living space, making it as immune as possible to extremes of outside temperature. The specific objective is to keep as even a temperature as possible on interior surfaces. Dead air is the most efficient insulating medium, so insulative materials are designed to trap air and hold it motionless. The more air the material holds still, the more efficient the insulator is. This efficiency is measured in terms of "R."

R stands for resistance to winter heat loss or summer heat gain. R-numbers or values are assigned to and stamped on all insulating materials. These values are rated on an ascending scale. The higher the R-number, the more effective the material.

Insulation installed above suspended ceiling systems will be in the form of batts or blankets, which are commonly composed of glass fiber or rock wool. Table 7-1 lists the R-values for these two materials.

Table 7-1: Common R-Values		
	Batts or Blankets	
R-Value	**Glass Fiber**	**Rock Wool**
R-11	2"—3-1/2"	3"
R-13	4"	4-1/2"
R-19	6"—6-1/2"	5-1/4"
R-22	6-1/2"	6"
R-26	8"	8-1/2"
R-30	9-1/2"—10-1/2"	9"
R-33	11"	10"
R-38	12"—13"	10-1/2"

Glass fiber and mineral wool products are generally safe from fire and toxic substances. They are also impervious to decomposition, moisture, and self-compaction. These characteristics make them a very desirable type of ceiling insulation.

Minimum recommended insulation requirements vary between geographic locations. Figure 7-26 shows R-values for all areas of the country.

Vapor Barrier

Humidity is a major factor in determining how effective insulation will be. Water droplets are contained within the air that is trapped and held motionless by the insulation. When cooler air is encountered, these droplets may condense. This condensation may damage the insulation and/or the ceiling panels themselves if the situation is severe enough. In order to prevent condensation and moisture-related damage, a vapor barrier must be installed.

	Ceilings	Walls	Floors
Zone A	R-44	R-19	R-22
Zone B	R-38	R-19	R-19
Zone C	R-30	R-19	R-19
Zone D	R-19	R-13	R-11
Zone E	R-19	R-11	R-11

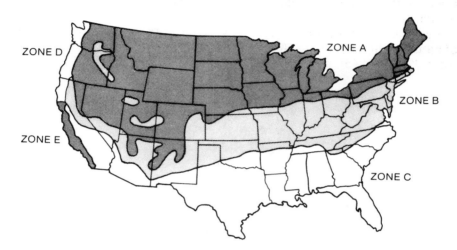

Fig. 7-26: *Regional insulation requirements.*

The vapor barrier must always be installed on the warm side of all exterior walls. In most homes, the interior of the building is warmer. The vapor barrier must then face inward. In suspended ceiling installations, this means the vapor barrier will be placed below the insulation. In many large buildings, such as supermarkets, the exterior of the building is warmer than the inside in both summer and winter. Air-conditioning runs during all seasons to offset the heat load of customers in the store. If the vapor barrier were facing inward in this case, condensation would form.

Plastic sheeting, 3 to 4 mils thick, is an effective vapor barrier. Install it so the edges overlap, forming an effective seal. The sheeting must extend to all walls and corners and be snugly attached. Tape shut all punctures or holes in the plastic.

Some batts and blankets have an attached vapor barrier. If paper or foil covered insulation must be used in conjunction with a plastic vapor barrier, the covering must be stripped off or slashed severely to destroy the barrier. Only one barrier may be used.

Insulation Installation

Insulation weighing up to 0.5 pound per square foot can easily be supported by a Chicago Metallic grid system. Installation is not overly complex. It is important to keep the insulation from depending on ceiling panels for support. Condensed moisture is also a concern when installing additional insulation. In order to avoid possible problems and/or ceiling damage, follow the recommendations given here.

The simplest and most effective way to avoid unnecessary weight distribution on ceiling panels is to lay latticework. Wall angles provide adequate lattice members. Angle lengths should be about 2' apart and positioned at a 45° angle to the grid (Fig. 7-27) to spread the weight evenly.

Next, determine the vapor barrier position, remembering to install the vapor barrier on the warm side of the insulation. Never use more than one vapor barrier.

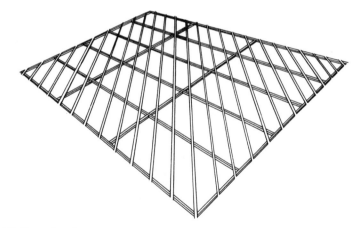

Fig. 7-27: *Wall angle placed across grid for support.*

If the warm side is the living area, proceed by placing plastic sheeting, 3 to 4 mils thick, across the top of the wall angle latticework. Make sure the vapor barrier sections overlap about 1' (Fig. 7-28). For the barrier to be effective, you must extend the plastic film to all walls and corners of the room. This treatment, when correctly and carefully finished, will help prevent moisture from condensing in acoustical material or wood. Condensation could lead to discoloration, warpage, etc.

The final phase is laying blankets or rolls of insulation over the vapor and latticework (Fig. 7-29). Always follow manufacturer's instructions and warnings given on the package. Choose an insulation suitable for

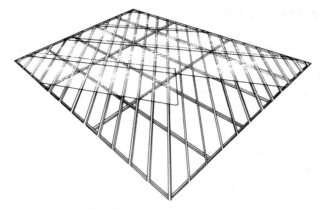

Fig. 7-28: *Vapor barrier is placed on the warm side of the installation.*

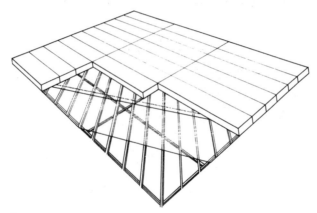

Fig. 7-29: *Insulating material is laid over the vapor barrier.*

your specific area. Many charts and pamphlets are available for information and guidelines.

If the warm side of the insulation is to the outside, reverse the process just described, laying the insulation first. *Note:* If the ceiling is installed with main runners every 2' and hanger wires at 3' intervals instead of the standard 4', even more insulation may be installed. The amount of insulation can be raised to roughly 1 pound per square foot.

STORAGE COMPARTMENTS

A suspended ceiling installation may easily be upgraded with the addition of a simple yet effective accessory—the storage compartment. The space above the suspended ceiling grid level functions as an insulator and screen for fixtures and ductwork. In most installations there is an abundance of unused air space which is readily adaptable for storage. The easy removal of panels permits unhindered access to the storage areas. In larger applications (or depending on the items stored), the area can be used in conjunction with Chicago Metallic Access Panel systems. The overhead, concealed storage area frees valuable floor and shelf space. Stowing seldom-used or seasonal items above ceiling level ensures dry, positive storage.

Such storage areas may be of two types. Both constructions are very similar. Before starting any type of construction, determine what the storage needs are. Take into consideration the size and shape of the stored item. Allow adequate space for ease of insertion and removal of stored objects. Remember to allow at least 3" of space between the bottom of the storage space and the ceiling panel level for panel removal and insertion.

The first type of storage compartment is the most basic and simplest to assemble. Utilizing the space between joists, such an arrangement provides storage for a number of items, depending on the building's construction characteristics. To determine how large the storage compartment must be, first determine the depth of the joist (Fig. 7-30). Next measure the distance between the outer edges of the joists. The remaining measurements are determined by the size of the object to be stored. The length of the object will determine the length of the compartment base. Make sure the height of the object does not exceed the joist depth. Mark off measurements B and C on a piece of 1/4" plywood (Fig. 7-31). Cut the plywood to size and attach with nails to the bottom of the

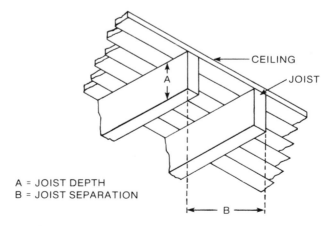

CEILING

JOIST

A = JOIST DEPTH
B = JOIST SEPARATION

B

Fig. 7-30: Measure the joists.

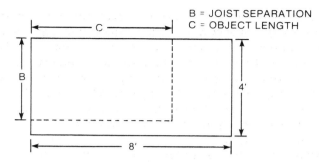

B = JOIST SEPARATION
C = OBJECT LENGTH

Fig. 7-31: *Cut plywood floor to size.*

joists. If more space is needed than available between joists, the bottom panel may be cut to extend over as many joists as necessary. Insert nails through the bottom panel into all joists to assure adequate support.

The second storage method will accommodate items with a greater depth than the ceiling joists. The sides are constructed in such a manner that the joists are extended. The amount of depth added will be determined again by the objects or materials to be stored. Remember to allow for the 3" minimum between the storage compartment's bottom and the

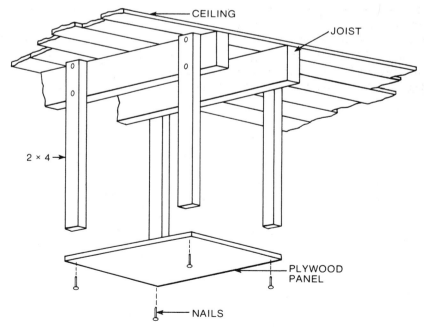

Fig. 7-32: *Larger items can be accommodated by 2 by 4 sides.*

ceiling level to permit insertion of the ceiling panels. To determine the depth of the side wall for the storage compartment, measure the length from the floorboards above the ceiling to the proposed storage floor. Cut 2 by 4s to this length, using a minimum of four (one for each corner) (Fig. 7-32). Additional members may be needed, depending on the weight of the stored objects.

The bottom is constructed in a method similar to the first storage compartment; however, 4" should be added to measurement B to accommodate the supporting 2 by 4s. Once the bottom has been measured and cut, the 2 by 4 supports should be fastened. Nail or screw through the plywood into the ends of the 2 by 4s. The storage compartment is now ready to hang. Nail the 2 by 4s to the appropriate ceiling joists and place the ceiling panels.

Now that the storage compartment is available for use, take care to select proper objects for storage. Advise your customers not to store flammable items such as paints and thinners above the ceiling. Their fumes may be trapped, presenting a potential hazard. Remember that temperatures are higher above the ceiling; avoid storing aerosol products or substances which may melt. A little common sense and thought will reduce the chance of creating a harmful situation.

FIRE RATED CEILINGS

Fire prevention and building code officials have two main concerns about suspended ceiling systems. The first is flame spread, or how fast the fire will spread on a material once a flame has touched the panel. This measurement is concerned with only the panels, not the grid.

Optimum protection from flame spread is provided by Class I, or non-combustible, materials. Such products are marked with a UL seal on the packaging, certifying the flame spread class.

The other fire code requirement is known as the hourly rating or time design. Again, this rating has nothing to do with the grid proper. Such requirements are mostly the concern of commercial construction. Simply, these tiles will impede the progress of a fire for a specified period of time. UL tests and assigns an hourly rating which will be found on the tile packaging.

In order that these fire rated tiles function correctly, consider two points. First, a fire rated grid must be used to suspend the tiles. A UL fire rating will mark such systems. This does not infer that the grid is stronger, but only that a special expansion feature is incorporated into the grid design. Expansion relief sections compensate for the effects of heat on the grid during a fire. Heated grid may buckle or sag, permitting tiles to fall from it and creating openings for the fire to reach above the ceiling.

The second fire prevention safety condition is fire rated fixture protection. The installation methods for a ducted fixture and a fixture that is not ducted will be outlined. These systems substantially reduce heat transmission through the ceiling during a fire. The fixtures illustrated are of the fluorescent tube type with steel housing. At least 1/2" heat diffusion space is required between the fixture housing and protective material. Installation conforms with the National Electric Code.

Non-Air Handling Fixture

The materials used for fire rated fabrication are to be UL classified. Mineral wool batts 1-1/4" thick, 5/8" acoustical material, or 1/2" or 5/8" gypsum wallboard may be used to fabricate the fixture covering.

The fixture in Fig. 7-33 is a 24" by 48" fluorescent light. In order to cover this fixture satisfactorily, a piece of material 30" by 60" must be laid out and cut as in Fig. 7-34. Cut two 6" by 6" spacers from the end of the pieces. Place the spacers approximately 6" from the end of the fixture (Fig. 7-33). Take care not to cover the ballast mounting surface. (Class P ballasts will prevent premature ballast failure due to overheating.)

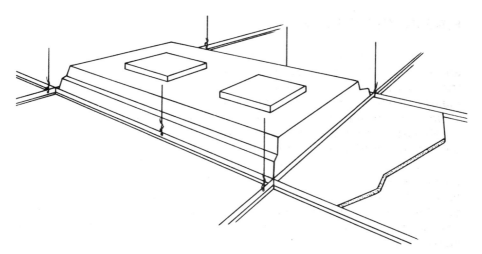

Fig. 7-33: *A 24" by 48" non-air handling fixture.*

Next, place the 4-1/2" by 48" side pieces against the fixture. Make sure these panels are on the inside of the cross tee. Now place the 21" by 48" top piece over the fixture body. This panel should be between the hanger wires resting on the spaces (Fig. 7-35).

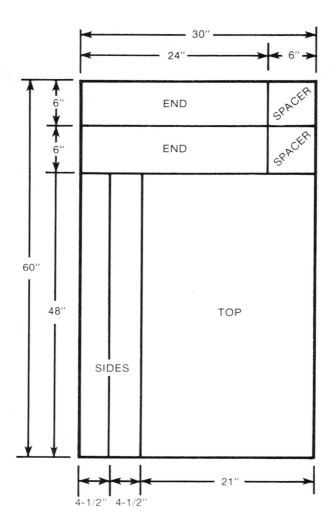

Fig. 7-34: *Cutting pattern for fire rated material.*

Stand the 6″ by 24″ end pieces loosely at each end. These pieces should rest perpendicularly to the fixture on the outside of the main runner (Fig. 7-36). If mineral wool was used, it should be secured with light gage wire. If acoustical tile or gypsum wallboard was used, secure the side and end pieces with 6d nails. Drive five nails along each end into the top and two at each end into the side pieces.

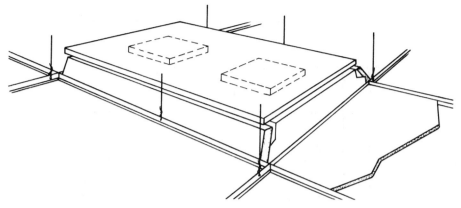

Fig. 7-35: *Placement of side pieces.*

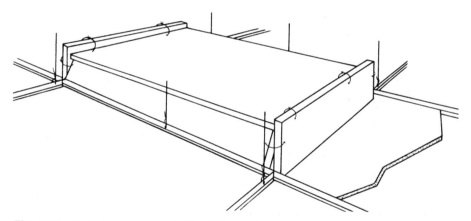

Fig. 7-36: *End pieces rest outside of the main runner.*

Air Handling Fixture

The procedure is similar for fabricating a fire rated covering for a non-air handling fixture. The sample fixture is 24″ by 48″. Dimensions and type of material must meet the same requirements as the previous installation. Always check the UL design for allowable light fixture protection material and construction details.

You will need a piece of material 48″ by 58″ to properly construct a fire rated cover. Cut this piece as shown in Fig. 7-37.

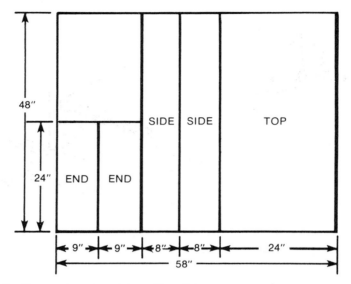

Fig. 7-37: *Cutting pattern for air handling fixture.*

Rest the 8" by 48" side pieces against the fixture sides (Fig. 7-38). Take care to place the batts on the inside of the cross tees. Cut the batt to fit snugly around the duct. Then place the 24" by 48" top piece over the fixture body between the hanger wires (Fig. 7-39).

Finally, place the end pieces loosely at each end (Fig. 7-40). These pieces should measure 9" by 24". The ends should rest almost perpendicularly to the fixture on the outside of the main runner. Fasten the materials together using the same methods mentioned for the non-air handling fixture.

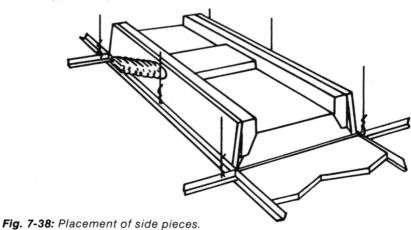

Fig. 7-38: *Placement of side pieces.*

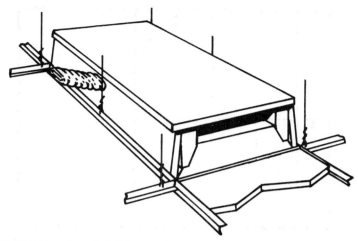

Fig. 7-39: *The top piece is laid onto the sides.*

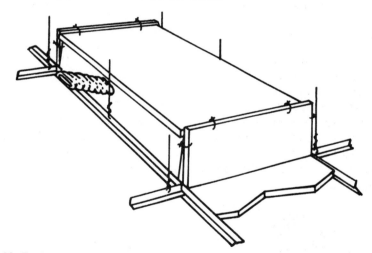

Fig. 7-40: *End pieces are fastened to the previously installed material.*

SMOKE AND HEAT DETECTOR INSTALLATION

An ever-increasing concern with fire safety has seen an increase in the number of detection devices installed in the home and required in light commercial installation. A suspended ceiling system is easily adapted to mount such devices.

To locate detectors, first consider their position within the room. Do not locate thermal or smoke detectors near corners or edges of walls. The manufacturer's instruction manual will provide specific requirements for various detection units. After determining the proper position, cut a 2 by 4 to fit between two main runners directly above the desired location. Leave the ceiling panel in the grid that will have the detector beneath it. Remove the panels on either side of it to provide easy access while installing the detection device. Insert screws through the main runners into the ends of the 2 by 4 to provide support for the unit. Remember to use additional hanger wires with any ceiling accessories.

Both thermal and smoke detectors are simply screw-mounted. Thermal detection units require that a hole be drilled through the panel and a supporting 2 by 4 to permit concealment of the circuit's wires. Mark the mounting screw holes and the wire hole location on the panel. Make sure the wire hole is completely concealed by the thermal unit. Drill the appropriate holes and insert screws to securely fasten the unit. A suspended ceiling provides an easy route for concealed wires, making an otherwise tricky installation quite simple.

Smoke detectors are probably the most common and popular safety feature being installed in homes today. Simply use the mounting plate as a template and mark the location for screw insertion. Drill starting holes through the panel into the supporting 2 by 4. Insert the screws and securely fasten the plate to the support. Insert batteries into the smoke detector and test the unit. Snap the working unit onto the mounting plate, and the installation is complete.

Use care and take time to carefully follow all manufacturer's warnings and instructions. Safety systems like thermal and smoke detection devices are effective only if correctly mounted. Proper installation can save the life of your customers.

CLEANING PANELS

Most smudges can be removed from the panel surface with an ordinary pencil or art gum eraser. If the panel requires more cleaning than this, be careful with the product finish. There are three basic finishes available for ceiling panels: cleanable, washable, and scrubbable.

Cleanable panels may be cleaned with a rubber sponge or wallpaper cleaner. Make sure the cleaning pad is fresh and unsoiled in order to prevent additional marking of the panel. Hide nicks and scratches with ordinary chalk. Remove dust and surface dirt by lightly brushing or vacuuming with a soft brush attachment. Cleanable panels should not be in contact with moisture of any kind; all cleaning should be dry. Acoustical mineral-fiber board is a typical example of a cleanable panel.

Panels which are washable may be slightly dampened. Water and mild detergent will remove most household marks. Use a sponge that has been wrung almost completely dry. Gently rub the area, making sure that the strokes are in the same direction as the panel texture or pattern. Do not excessively moisten or soak panels; this will permanently harm the finish. Cellulose or panels of a similar material are washable.

Some panels may have either an acrylic or plastic finish applied at the factory. These panels are referred to as scrubbable. Clean them exactly like washable panels. The special finishes on these panels will, however, take gentle scrubbing with a soft bristle brush if necessary.

Luminous panels, such as those covering fluorescent lighting fixtures, are composed entirely of plastic. These panels may be soaked and vigorously scrubbed. Take care if any cleaning agent other than detergent and water is used. Certain plastics will react undesirably when they come in contact with petroleum-based products.

Warn your customers not to hang heavy objects from the ceiling. They can, however, hang lightweight paper party decorations or holiday decorations. Always hang from the grid components and not from the ceiling panels. Use removable tape or plastic hooks so as not to damage the finish.

THE FINISHED CEILING AND YOUR CUSTOMER

After the installation is completed, demonstrate ceiling maintenance procedures to the customer. Take time to remove a panel and cover the cleaning methods that apply to the particular tile. Review any special accessories, special features, and improper uses of the grid and explain the suspended ceiling advantages. Since your knowledge and advice may be called upon after the installation, offer to answer any future questions and leave your card. This extra 15 minutes of instruction may lead to valuable word-of-mouth advertising and future business.

Throughout this book, Chicago Metallic Corporation has endeavored to provide contractors with a basic working knowledge necessary to complete residential and light commercial grid installations. The most important advice we can give the contractor is a reminder that an installation involves more than just hanging components from wire and dropping tile in place. The ability to explain the hows and whys of suspended ceilings is the mark of an expert contractor. From planning to placing the last tile is simply a matter of following the guidelines and sticking to them.

We at Chicago Metallic would like to hear from you. If you have any questions, comments, ideas, or problems, contact the CMC office nearest you.

GLOSSARY

Acoustical—Refers to the sound absorbing character of a ceiling tile or panel. Acoustical panels will not reflect more than 50% of the sound striking them.

Astralite—These 2' by 2' steel ceiling light panels and solid decorator panels are coated in either brass, chrome, white, architectural bronze, or sandstone to accent any decor.

Aviation Snips—Specially geared metal cutting tool used for cutting or trimming of main runner, cross tee, and molding sections.

Bulb—The top of a main runner or cross tee web, resulting from the folding of steel sheeting.

Cellulose Fiber—The generic term indicating organic composition of a material. Ceiling panels may be compressed wood fiber or bagasse (sugar cane stalk).

Chalk Line—Used to mark long straight lines on walls or other surfaces for reference use in construction. It is made by using a taut string coated with colored chalk powder which, when snapped against a surface, will transfer a straight line to the surface.

Cleanable—The type of finish on a ceiling panel which may only be cleaned by a dry method.

Cross Tee—The intermediate supports of a suspended ceiling system. These grid members lock into slots in the main runner and/or other cross tees.

Deburr—The process of removing distorted (burred) edges from cut metal by using a metal file to smooth roughened edges.

Ducts—Usually large round or rectangular tubes used to distribute air from the furnace or air-conditioning to the rooms. They may be constructed of various materials.

Electrogalvanizing—A special zinc-based process which electrically undercoats steel before painting. This undercoating resists rusting of the steel.

Fire Resistance Classification—Numerical time ratings derived under controlled laboratory conditions which measure the ability of a ceiling to prevent the spread of flame and hot gases through the construction to the level above. This provides protection for the structural elements to prevent early collapse. Ratings may not be predictive of the assembly's performance under actual fire conditions.

Flame Spread Classification—The numerical index calculated under laboratory conditions which measures the flame spread across the face of a ceiling material. Various products are identically tested, though the number may not be predictive of a material's performance in an actual fire.

Flange—The front leg of a wall molding, which will be parallel to the floor and ceiling when installed. The unpunched leg of a wall molding.

Hanger Wire—Used to suspend the grid from the overhead structure, supporting the bulk of the ceiling weight. Extra hanger wires should be added whenever anything other than a panel will be supported by the ceiling grid.

Hold-Down Clip—A securing device that keeps panels snug in the grid.

Joists—Wooden structure supports for the roof or floor above the room in which a suspended ceiling might be installed. Joists are made of 2" lumber and are normally spaced 16" on center. Screw eyes or nails to hold hanger wires for a suspended ceiling are attached here.

Leg—The two sides of a wall molding. The back leg is that which has prepunched holes. The front leg is referred to as the flange.

Main Runners—These are the long supporting members of the ceiling grid, sometimes called beams. Main runners are supported by wire from overhead. Slots for cross tees to lock into are located on the main runners.

Mineral Fiber—The general designation applied to ceiling products manufactured from mineral fibers, bonded and formed by felting, and heat cured.

Mitered Cut—Two cut angles whose joint causes a section of wall molding to turn a corner or change direction.

Molding—Grid member which attaches to the walls of a room at the level of the new ceiling. Made of a thin ribbon of metal bent longitudinally at a 90° angle, it provides support for the ceiling at the walls.

Panels—These are similar to ceiling tiles in that they are finished and patterned on the side which faces the room. Panels are larger than tiles, generally 24" by 24" or 24" by 48", and have plain, ungrooved edges. They are designed to lay in a suspended ceiling grid to make a ceiling.

Perspective Drawing—A sketch of a building taken from a particular vantage point. Height, width, and depth are shown along with enough detail that a photograph from the same position would be similar.

Pocket Estimator—A sliding card sleeve device used by counter and sales personnel to help quickly estimate the approximate amount of materials required to make a ceiling for a room of a given size.

Reference Strings—A key to accurate installation of a suspended ceiling. There are two types of reference strings: the first shows the position of the main runners; the second is used to trim the main runners so that the cross tees will be in their proper locations.

R-Value—The numerical measure of thermal resistance, per unit area, for a particular material(s). The higher the R-value, the greater the resistance to heat flow.

Scrubbable—Describes a panel finish which may be dampened with water and a mild detergent. The panel surface will accept gentle scrubbing with a soft bristled brush.

Slots—Vertical openings in the main runner into which cross tee ends are inserted and locked.

Splice—The device used to link two main runners together.

Splicing—The procedure by which main runners are interconnected to form a continuous member for ceiling support down the length of the room.

Splice Tab—A securing device which, when folded down, lock sections of main runner together.

Trim—Cutting steel grid members to fit accurately in place. Important at walls where main runners and cross tees must rest securely on the full flange.

Vapor Barrier—A moistureproof sheet laid separately or preattached to the insulation. It is always installed on the warm side of an area to provide optimum insulative properties.

Wall Angle—See molding.

Washable—Describes a ceiling panel finish which may be cleaned with water and mild detergent. A sponge squeezed nearly dry should be used, wiping in the same direction of the pattern or texture.

Web—The metal ribbon perpendicular to the main runner flange on which prepunched holes are located.

Index

NOTES

Chapter 1 _____

_____

_____

_____

Chapter 2 _____

_____

_____

_____

Chapter 3 _____

_____

_____

_____

Chapter 4 _____

_____

_____

_____

Chapter 5 _____

_____

_____

_____

_____

Chapter 6 _____

_____

_____

_____

_____

Chapter 7 _____

_____

_____

_____

_____

$**5**.⁰⁰ OFFER FROM

CHICAGO METALLIC CORPORATION

Get a $5 rebate on your first purchase of $50 or more of Chicago Metallic ceiling grid systems or Astralite™ lights or panels. Here's all you do:

- Complete information requested below.
  Cut coupon from book and attach it to **store receipt** or facsimile, and **include proof of purchase** (grid: a 1″ section of flattened grid; Astralite: the words, "Chicago Metallic Corporation" from **both** end flaps of the carton).

- Mail to:

  Remodeler's Guide Book Redemption
  Chicago Metallic Corporation
  4849 South Austin Avenue
  Chicago, IL 60638

- Only one rebate per customer. Offer void where prohibited by law. *Rebate offer expires Dec. 31, 1985.*

- -

My purchase was made at ☐ hardware store   ☐ lumber retailer
☐ home center   ☐ other_____

My installation is ☐ residential   ☐ commercial
☐ institutional   ☐ other_____

My project will be installed by ☐ owner   ☐ contractor

I am a ☐ homeowner   ☐ contractor

Mail rebate check to:

Name _____

Address _____

City _____ State _____ ZIP _____

- -

Chicago Metallic Corporation

Chicago Metallic Corporation is the nation's premier manufacturer of ceiling suspension systems. We offer a wide selection of grid systems and accessories. In a variety of finishes and colors. Backed up with service that's helped make us the industry leader.

This installation book is just one example of Chicago Metallic's responsiveness to the needs of remodelers. We constantly are refining our products. Developing new systems to take advantage of improved materials and installation techniques. Offering products that match the latest trends in design and decorating.

For more information or product specifications see our insert in Sweets Catalog. Or contact the Chicago Metallic representative nearest you.

4849 South Austin Avenue, Chicago, IL 60638
6750 Santa Barbara Court, Baltimore, MD 21227
5501 Downey, Los Angeles, CA 90058